THE FUNDAMENTAL UNITY OF INDIA

THE FUNDAMENTAL UNITY OF INDIA

(FROM HINDU SOURCES)

BY

RADHAKUMUD MOOKERJI, M.A.

WITH AN INTRODUCTION BY

J. RAMSAY MACDONALD, M.P.

GYAN

Published by

Gyan Publishing House
5, Ansari Road
Daryaganj, New Delhi-110002
Phone: 011-47034999, 9811692060
E-mail: books@gyanbooks.com

Distribution Network
gyanbooks.com
India, USA, Canada, UK, Australia

ISBN: 978-93-6208-537-5 (PB)
First Published, 1914

2nd Impression 2024

Printed at: Gyan Press, Delhi.

THE FUNDAMENTAL UNITY OF INDIA
Author: RADHAKUMUD MOOKERJI

THE FUNDAMENTAL UNITY OF INDIA

(FROM HINDU SOURCES)

BY

RADHAKUMUD MOOKERJI, M.A.

Premchand Roychand Scholar, Calcutta University; Hemchandra Basu Mallik Professor of Indian History in the National Council of Education, Bengal; Author of "A History of Indian Shipping and Maritime Activity from the Earliest Times," &c., &c.

WITH AN INTRODUCTION BY

J. RAMSAY MACDONALD, M.P.

LONGMANS, GREEN AND CO.

39, PATERNOSTER ROW, LONDON

NEW YORK, BOMBAY, AND CALCUTTA

1914

TO

THE PROMOTERS OF

THE HINDU UNIVERSITY OF BENARES

FOR THEIR NOBLE EFFORTS TOWARDS THE

CONSERVATION AND DEVELOPMENT

OF

HINDU LEARNING AND CULTURE

IN THE SERVICE OF HUMANITY.

"अहं सर्वेषां राज्ञां श्रैष्ठ्यमतिष्ठां परमतांगच्छेयं साम्राज्यं भौज्यं स्वाराज्यं पारमेष्ठ्यं राज्यं माहाराज्यं आधिपत्यं अहं समन्तपर्यायीस्यां सार्वभौमः सार्वायुष आन्तादापरार्धात् पृथिव्यै समुद्रपर्यन्ताया एकराडिति ।"

—*Aitareya Brāhmaṇa*, [VIII. i. 39.]

["It is my desire to attain to superiority, pre-eminence and overlordship among all kings, to acquire an all-embracing authority by achieving all forms and degrees of sovereignty, to achieve the conquest of both space and time and be the sole monarch of the earth up to the seas."]

से च पुन लधे देवानां पियस च सवेस च अतेसु असषु पिच्छाजने सेचो सतस अते अन्तियोगे नाम योन पलन च तेन अन्तियोजेना चतुलि लाजने तुलमये नाम अनेकिन नाम मक नाम अलिक्यसदले नाम निचं चोद पाण्ड्या अवं तम्वपन्निया हेवमेव हेवमेव पादालाजा विसम्वसि योन कवजेसु नावकनाभपंक्तिसु भोज पिटिनि-क्येसु अन्धपलन्देसु सवता देवानां पियस धम्मानुसथि अनुवतन्ति ।—*Asoka Rock Edict* xiii.

["And this is the chiefest conquest in the opinion of His Sacred Majesty—the Conquest of Dharma—and this conquest, again, has been won by His Sacred Majesty both in his own dominions and in all the neighbouring realms as far as six hundred leagues—where the Greek King Antiochos dwells, and north of that Antiochos to where dwell the four great kings severally named Ptolemy, Antigonos, Magas and Alexander; and in the south (the realms of the) Cholas, and Pāndyas, with Ceylon likewise—and here, too, in the King's dominions, among the Yonas and Kāmbojas, among the Nābhapantis of Nābhaka, among the Bhojas and Pitinikas, among the Āndhras and Pulindas."]

PREFACE

THIS brochure is based on an article which I contributed to the *Dawn and Dawn Society's Magazine* in January, 1909. In its present form it was delivered as an address to the Calcutta University Institute in March last under the presidency of Sir Gooroodass Banerji, Kt., M.A., D.L., Ph.D., Ex-Vice-Chancellor of the Calcutta University; and it was reproduced in the pages of *The Modern Review* for April. It is now published with several additions and alterations.

In this work I have not dwelt upon the important evidence of the fundamental unity of India furnished by the social and religious institutions of the country, but have confined my attention mainly to its geographical basis.

I am deeply indebted to Dr. Brajendranath Seal, M.A., Ph.D., King George V. Professor of Philosophy of the Calcutta University, for many valuable suggestions I received from him.

Mr. Nundolal Dey, M.A., B.L., the author of "A Geographical Dictionary of Ancient and Mediæval India," has also laid me under great obligation by preparing for the book a Map of Ancient India. My thanks are also due to the Hon. Pandit Madanmohon Malaviya for kindly revising the proofs.

My grateful acknowledgments are due to the Hon. Maharaja Manindra Chandra Nandy of Cossimbazar for the generous support he has accorded to me in the preparation of this work.

RADHAKUMUD MOOKERJI.

BERHAMPORE (BENGAL),
August, 1913.

INTRODUCTION

Mr. Radhakumud Mookerji has honoured me by asking me to write an introduction to his interesting book. To those who follow the work of the band of Indian historical students who are struggling, with no great measure of encouragement, to found a school native to the soil and inspired by Indian tradition, Mr. Mookerji's books need no introduction, especially since he published his *History of Indian Shipping*. In this little book he attempts to lay the only foundation upon which an Indian Historical School can rest. If India is a mere geographical expression, a mere collection of separate peoples, traditions, and tongues existing side by side but with no sense of nationhood in common,

Indian history cannot be the record of an evolution of a civilization—it can be nothing more than an account of raids, conflicts, relations of conquerors and conquered. That this is the common view is only too true; that a superficial view of India lends all its weight to that view is only too apparent; that it is the view of many of the present governors is proclaimed without secrecy from Ceylon to Afghanistan.

Those who read this book will find that there is another view, and that the Hindu, at any rate, from his traditions and his religion, regards India not only as a political unit naturally the subject of one sovereignty—whoever holds that sovereignty, whether British, Mohammedan, or Hindu—but as the outward embodiment, as the temple—nay, even as the goddess mother—of his spiritual culture. India and Hinduism are organically related as body and soul. Nationality is at best a difficult thing to define, to test and establish. The barren controversies on the subject to which the demands of Ireland for Home Rule have led, prove that. But the Aryan settled it decisively so far as India and himself are concerned. He made India the symbol of his culture; he filled it with his soul. In his consciousness it was his greater self. How he did it Mr. Mookerji shows in his interesting chapters.

Mr. Mookerji writes only of history, but it is a history which we read with political thoughts in our mind. It is this history quickened into life which is giving us our Indian political problems. What share has the Mohammedan in it? Perhaps much greater than we think. The *Pax Britannica* does not merely shelter weak men; it is also a shade under which liberal political ideas take root and flourish. And nationalism cannot be dissociated from liberal political ideas. To amplify and discuss this would be out of place here, and Mr. Mookerji would not wish me to use the privileges of an introduction to widen until it passes into current political controversy the historical field of his study. But these thoughts have been in my mind as they will no doubt be in that of everyone who reads this book, and I have been anxious to indicate that in my opinion, at any rate, the unity of India will not remain exclusively a Hindu conception, although its origin may be in Hindu culture.

Many people imagine that this Indian nationhood is only a disturbing element in politics. But that is a mistake. It is a reviving influence on culture. Indeed, in some respects, its political expressions are its crudest and most ill-formed embodiments. We have it best—if, as yet, in no very great volume—in art and literature. In art, as in education, we have been proclaiming, in our vanity, that India had to learn the Western tone and touch, with the result that Indian art has been debased and every spontaneous thought crushed out of it. But life returned through the nationalist revival. Nothing has ever struck me with more force than the contrast between the ugly daubs which compose an art exhibition in India held under Western auspices and the product of Western "inspiration" on the one hand, and the beautiful harmonies of form and colour which the Indian Art Society brings together on the other. And it is interesting to note how in this art the spirit of India is not merely Hindu. Mr. Tagore's great painting "The Death of Shah Jehan," is as essentially Persian as his "Spirit of India" is Hindu. Moreover, in literature, are we not at present in the midst of a "Gitanjali" puja—all unconscious that it is the refined expression of Indian nationalism? Finally, there are the students of intellectual culture with whom Mr. Mookerji himself co-operates, gathering together the scattered records of Indian achievement so that they may be known and due homage paid to the people who accomplished them. Thus India awakes anew to a sense of independence and self-respect, and only by such an awakening can she contribute her share to the culture of the world.

J. RAMSAY MACDONALD.

THE ARGUMENT

I. *The primary factor of Nationality is the possession of a common country—a common fatherland is preliminary to all national development—the formation of an Indian nation must wait on the realisation by the Indians of the whole of India as their common mother country, claiming their loyalty and service.*

II. *But is India a single country? Difference of opinion among European and Anglo-Indian scholars.*

III. *The geographical unity of India is easily missed in her immensity and variety—an account of India's vastness and variety—the variety only contributes to her wealth and strength and economic self-sufficiency.*

IV. *To superficial observation the whole is lost in the parts—the fundamental unity of India is, however, acknowledged by many competent authorities.*

V. *But this unity is generally traced to the influence of British rule in India—it has really a long history, and has been an element in the historic consciousness of the Hindus from a remote age—the oldest expression of this unity was the name Bhāratavarṣa, which the ancient Hindus applied to India—the full significance of the name indicating the Aryanisation of India.*

VI.–VII. *Further expressions of the old Hindu consciousness of Indian geographical unity in the Vedic and subsequent literature—the river-hymn of the 'Ṛig-Veda' and its epic adaptation with expanding geographical horizon—other later hymns which have passed into national daily prayers—their effects on popular consciousness in awakening it to a sense of the individuality and sacredness of the whole of India from end to end.*

VIII. *The feeling for the fatherland finds frequent expression in Sanskrit literature.*

IX. *A permanent and characteristically Indian expression of this feeling is in the network of shrines and sacred places by which the country has been covered—the institution of pilgrimage as an expression of love for the motherland, of appreciation of Art and Nature—pilgrimage as a means of acquiring an intimate knowledge of the country in olden times before the era of modern travelling facilities—the lists of Hindu holy places in Sanskrit literature show complete familiarity with every part of India.*

X. *Corresponding to the Hindu expression of love for the motherland is the Buddhist expression of the feeling in the multitude of monuments with which it beautified the whole country—enumeration of these monuments showing the vast area unified by a common impulse.*

XI. *The geographical knowledge of the whole of India and, consequently, the perception of its unity was itself the development of centuries.*

XII. *History of the development of this knowledge—the geographical horizon in the Vedic age—the extension of the limits of Vedic India in the 'Aitareya Brāhmaṇa.'*

XIII. *Probable period of the colonisation of Southern India—evidences from Paṇini and oldest Pali texts—the geographical horizon between the Vedic and early Buddhist periods.*

XIV. *The whole of India was known at least as early as the fourth century* B.C.*—the evidence of Kātyāyana—Greek evidence—the geographical data in the 'Arthaśāstra' of Kauṭilya—the geography of the Asoka Edicts.*

XV. *The geography of Patañjali* (150 B.C.)*—of the Rāmāyana—and of the Mahābhārata.*

XVI. *The geography of the Purāṇas—of the Bṛihatsaṅhitā of Varāhamihira, showing an intimate knowledge of all parts of India.*

XVII. *The geography of Kālidāsa—end of the account of the development of Indian geographical knowledge.*

XVIII. *The sense of the unity of the whole country was promoted, not only by religion as shown above, but also by politics—rulers of India who established their sway over the whole country, and consequently contemplated and used it as a unit—the oldest of them is generally thought to be Chandragupta.*

XIX. *But the institution of paramount sovereignty was much older than Chandragupta—it was a familiar political idea of the ancient Hindus—evidence on the subject—the terms for a paramount sovereign in Vedic literature.*

XX. *The 'Aitareya Brāhmaṇa' and 'Śukranīti' on the grades of kingly power—the Vedic terms for overlordship.*

XXI. *Further Vedic evidence — the ceremonies specifically fixed for the coronations of emperors—significance of the details and procedure of the Vājapeya.*

XXII. *Significance of the details of the Rājasūya.*

XXIII. *Significance of the imperial inaugurations as described in the 'Aitareya Brāhmaṇa.'*

XXIV. *The ideal of Hindu kingship was nothing short of universal sovereignty, which meant at the least sovereignty of the whole of India "up to the seas"—the consciousness of the territorial synthesis leads to the political synthesis, and is itself strengthened by the latter.*

XXV. *Ideals of an all-India overlordship are, however, preserved in Sanskrit literature, along with their concrete embodiments—lists of such paramount kings—in the 'Aitareya Brāhmaṇa'—in the 'Śatapatha Brāhmaṇa'—in the 'Śāṅkhāyana Sutra.'*

XXVI. *The lists of such kings in the Purāṇas—in the Mahābhārata—the Arthaśāstra on the conception of an all-India overlord.*

XXVII. *The conquests of the Pāṇḍavas leading to the establishment of their paramount sovereignty under Yudhiṣṭhira—the resulting political unification of India*

XXVIII. *Popularisation of the idea of an all-India sovereignty through the story of Yudhiṣṭhira—the current Hindu political notion of a Chakravarttī Rāja has shaped early Buddhist speculation about the true position and work of the Buddha—the Buddha was the spiritual sovereign who ruled supreme over the empire of righteousness in the hearts of men.*

XXIX. *Thus the sovereignty of Chandragupta Maurya was only a further stage in the development of an old institution—the idea became a common topic of discussion in the works on Hindu Polity—treatment of the* *problem, "How can a king become a king of kings?" in our Ńiti-Śāstras—the conception of the balance of power in a political system or sphere described therein.*

XXX. *The evidence of Inscriptions as to the strength and popularity of the ideal of a paramount sovereignty governing the whole of India.*

XXXI. *Another conclusive evidence bearing on the popular realisation of Indian unity is the Indian colonisations resulting in the development of a Greater India across the seas.*

XXXII. *Besides the historical factor, there are physical factors in constant operation which establish the geographical unity of India—comparison of the barriers which separate its internal parts from those that separate it from the surrounding external countries—the effects of the monsoons in creating uniform physical conditions.*

XXXIII. *The destiny and message of India.*

THE FUNDAMENTAL UNITY OF INDIA

(from Hindu Sources)

I

THERE are various elements necessary in the making of a nation such as a common language, a common religion, a common government and a common culture and social economy, but perhaps the most fundamental and indispensable factor is the possession of a common country, a fixed, definite abode. Even nationality has a material physical basis without which it can hardly manifest and assert itself as a real existence and factor in the political world. History shows no authentic record of nomadic peoples developing to any great extent in civilisation until and unless they bound themselves to a fixed habitation and rid themselves of their migratory instincts and habits. The Hebrew people, in spite of the political training they received from Moses, could not achieve much progress until Joshua settled them in Palestine. So also what the histórians call the Dark Age of Europe is but the period of unrest and transition when the barbarians left their old homes, overran and disorganised the Roman Empire, but were themselves without any fixed local habitation. "The Athenians under Themistocles saved the State of Athens on their ships, because after the victory they again took possession of their city; but the Teutones and Cimbri perished, because they left their old homes and failed to conquer a new one."

The spirit, according to Hindu philosophy, clothes itself in the body in and through which it works; it needs a vehicle, an instrument, a physical framework whereby it expresses and outshapes itself in the external world of matter. And it seems that the same principle applies in respect of the spirit of nationality. The primary requisite for the birth and growth of a nation is the certainty, fixity and permanence of *place*, and when *that* is assured the other formative forces will appear and make themselves felt in due course. A common fatherland is preliminary to all national development: round that living nucleus will naturally gather all those feelings, associations, traditions, and other elements which go to make up a people's language and literature, religion and culture, and thereby establish its separate existence and individuality, demanding its preservation and independent development as a valuable cultural unit. The unifying influence of a common country, of common natural surroundings is indeed irresistible, and the assertion may be safely made that it will be effectively operative against other disintegrating, disruptive forces and tendencies such as differences in manners and customs, language and religion.

The formation of a composite, federal Indian nation is one of the most interesting of modern political possibilities because of the great and unusual difficulties surrounding that movement. But the very first step towards the solution of those difficulties is clearly the cognisance of the fundamental fact that the diverse races and peoples making up the vast mass of Indian humanity cannot be welded together into a living nation, a puissant political force, unless in the first place they can understand and feel that they have a common country to love and to serve, that they all belong to one motherland, that they are all children of the same soil. Without this expanded geographical consciousness in the people the cherished dreams of the impatient political idealist about an Indian nation in the making will ever be remote from realisation.

II

But unfortunately it has become by no means easy to think of India as a single country. No picture of India is now more familiar to the Indian mind than that which represents it to be a continent, or a collection of *many* countries rather than *one* country. For this is the picture that is drawn in most of the standard works on Indian Geography taught in our schools. An English author of a geography for Indian schools introduces his book with the following remarks: "India is commonly thought of and spoken of as a single country. But this is not true . . . . India is rather a collection of countries." According to Sir John Strachey, the great Anglo-Indian authority, "this is the first and most essential thing to learn about India—that there is not and never was an India or even any country of India, possessing, according to European ideas, any sort of unity, physical, political . . . ." But Anglo-Indian opinion itself is however by no means unanimous on this point. Mr. Vincent A. Smith, the well-known authority on early Indian History, has delivered himself in a quite different strain: "India, encircled as she is by seas and mountains, is indisputably a geographical unit, and as such is rightly designated by one name." Equally positive and emphatic are the following words of Chisholm, one of the best known authorities on Geography: "There is no part of the world better marked out by Nature as a region by itself than India, exclusive of Burma. It is a region indeed full of contrasts in physical features and in climate, — but the features that divide it as a whole from surrounding regions are too clear to be overlooked."

III

The fact is that the geographical unity of India is apt to be lost sight of in her immensity and variety. It is difficult to imagine the vast territory that stretches from North to South over a distance exceeding 2,000 miles and from East to West over a distance of more than 1,900 miles as one continuous territory. The total area included within its limits is about two-thirds of that of the continent of Europe. It is nearly fourteen times as large as Great Britain and over ten times the size of the entire British Isles. It is more than six times the area of either France or Germany. This immensity of her geographical extension has naturally induced those physical conditions which have made of India pre-eminently the land of varieties, 'the epitome of the world.' It is the land, primarily, of as many latitudes as altitudes. The temperature ranges from the singularly dry and bracing cold of the Himalayas culminating in eternal snows to the humid, tropical heat of the Konkan and Coromandel coast. The surface rises from the sea-level to heights above the limits of vegetation, above cloud and rain and storm, merged in eternal sunshine. Its climates vary, on the one hand, from torrid and tropical to arctic and polar including between the extremes various shades of the mean or temperate, and, on the other, from almost absolute aridity to a maximum of humidity. The rainfall ranges from 460 inches at Cherrapoonjee to less than even 3 inches in Upper Sind. This amazing variety of latitudes and altitudes, temperature and moisture, produces a corresponding variety in flora and fauna. The range of climatic zones determines that of Botanical as well as Zoological zones. Thus, according to Sir J. D. Hooker,[1] the flora of India is more varied than that of any other country of equal area in the eastern hemisphere, if not in the globe. As regards the richness of the Indian fauna, the following testimony of Mr. Blandford[2] is sufficient: "Animal life is not only abundant in British India, but it is remarkably varied. The number of kinds of animals inhabiting India and its dependencies is very large, far surpassing, for instance, that of the species found in the whole of Europe, although the superficial area of Europe exceeds that of the Indian Empire by about one-half." This extraordinary richness and variety of the flora and fauna of India necessarily imply a corresponding richness and variety in her vegetable and animal products, endowing her with a degree of economic self-sufficiency which falls to

[1] *Imperial Gazetteer*, new ed., Vol. I., p. 157.
[2] *Ibid*, p. 213.

the lot of but few countries in the world. As Mr. Lilly puts it, the products of India 'include everything needed for the service of man.' But scarcely less than this physical variety is the *human* variety which India presents with her teeming millions. They absorb so much as a fifth of the whole human race, including races and peoples belonging to all stages and states of social evolution and civilisation with languages, manners and customs, cults and cultures of the most diverse kinds. There are in India no less than seven main physical types of races introducing varieties of physical form in the population; no less than fourteen separate peoples or nationalities with their own languages and literature; no less than 150 different tongues producing a veritable Babel of languages[1]; and, finally, nearly

[1] According to Dr. Cust, "no less than 539 languages and dialects, cultivated and uncultivated, in the whole of India and its bordering regions."

all the world-religions, each claiming more than a million of worshippers. India is verily a museum of cults and customs, creeds and cultures, faiths and tongues, racial types and social systems.

IV

Superficial observers are therefore liable to be bewildered by this astonishing variety in Indian life and geography. They lack that power of perception which dives beneath appearances and externals and sees into the life of things. They thus fail to discover the One in the Many, the Individual in the Aggregate, the Simple in the Composite. With them, the whole is lost in the parts, nay, the parts are greater than the whole, as in the old adage of blind men 'seeing' the elephant. The fact is that an exclusive dependence upon mere sense-impressions, mere sense-contact with external phenomena, cannot carry us very far: for the senses cannot take us beyond the apparent and the objective. What is needed is the superior interpreting, integrating, synthetising power of the mind that instead of being overpowered by the multitude of details will master them and rise above them to a vision of the whole.

A keen, penetrating insight can hardly fail to recognise that beneath all this manifold variety there is a fundamental unity; that this diversity itself, far from being a source of weakness, is a fertile source of strength and wealth. As Sir Herbert Risley has truly observed: "Beneath the manifold diversity of physical and social type, language, custom and religion which strikes the observer in India there can still be discerned, as Mr. Yusuf Ali has pointed out, a certain underlying uniformity[1] of life from the Himalayas to Cape Comorin." The last Indian Census Commissioner, Mr. E. A. Gait, I.C.S., has also recorded the same conclusion: "The people of India as a whole can be distinguished from those of Europe by certain broad characteristics." While, according to Mr. Vincent A. Smith, speaking from his long and first-hand experience of India, the civilisation of India "has many features which differentiate it from that of all other regions of the world; while they are

[1] One aspect of this unity has been thus explained by Monier Williams (*Hinduism*, page 13): "India, though it has, as we have seen, more than 500 spoken dialects, has only one sacred language and only one sacred literature, accepted and revered by all adherents of Hinduism alike, however diverse in race, dialect, rank, and creed. That language is Sanskrit, and that literature is Sanskrit literature—the only repository of the Veda or 'knowledge' in its widest sense; the only vehicle of Hindu theology, philosophy, law and mythology; the only mirror in which all the creeds, opinions, customs, and usages of the Hindus are faithfully reflected; and (if we may be allowed a fourth metaphor) the only quarry whence the requisite materials may be obtained for improving the vernaculars or for expressing important religious and scientific ideas."

common to the whole country or rather continent in a degree sufficient to justify its treatment as a unit in the history of human social and intellectual development."

V

It is generally recognised and admitted on all hands that this Indian unity is largely, if not solely, the creation of the British rule, a by-product of the Pax Britannica, the inevitable outcome of a centralised administration which controls the whole country from the Himalayas to Cape Comorin. What is not generally known and recognised, however, is that the idea of this fundamental unity is much older than British rule, that it is not a recent growth or discovery but has a history running back to a remote antiquity. There are many proofs to show that the great founders of Indian religion, culture and civilisation were themselves fully conscious of the geographical unity of their vast mother country and sought in various ways to impress it on the popular consciousness.

The first expression they appear to have given to this sense of unity was their description of the entire country by the single name of Bhāratavarṣa,[1] which is the old indigenous classic name by which India was known to the Hindus. For the name India was given to the country by foreigners. The river Sindhu by which the country was first known to

[1] India was originally called *Jambudvīpa.* This name was in use even in the time of Asoka who, in Buddhist works, is often styled as the king of Jambudvīpa. Some of the Pāla kings also style themselves as Kings of *Jambudvīpa* in their inscriptions. While the name *Jambudvīpa* has a geographical reference, the name Bhāratavarṣa has a political reference conveying the idea that the whole of India was governed by a single king (see the Purāṇas for the etymological significance of the word). Though Jambudvīpa and Bhāratavarṣa were no doubt names applied to the region conquered or colonised by the Aryans, yet subsequent additions by conquest were also known by those general names, as accretions to the main land are known by the name of the latter.

outsiders was changed into Hindu by the Persians, and Indos by the Greeks, dropping the hard aspirate. The name Bhāratavarṣa is not a mere geographical expression like the term India, having only a physical reference. It has a deep, historical significance symbolising a fundamental unity which was certainly perceived and understood by those who invented the name. It is a well-known doctrine of logic that when a common name is applied to different things, it is because of some principle of unity which connects them to a system in spite of the differences. It was hence a consciousness of unity that really made the Ṛiṣis of old to apply a single, individualising, appellation to a vast stretch of territory with parts divided by endless varieties and peopled by many races speaking many dialects, professing many faiths, owning many cultures. Bhāratavarṣa is derived from Bharata as Rome is derived from Romulus. Bharata is a great hero of Indian history and tradition, just as Romulus is of Roman. The *Ṛig-Veda*[1] first mentions him as the leader of a powerful Aryan tribe that played its full part in the original struggles and conflicts by which Aryan polity and culture were being shaped into proper form in the dawn of Indian history. The *Āitarēya Brāhmaṇa*[2] refers to his coronation ceremony and subsequent career of conquests leading to his overlordship which is duly solemnised by the performance of the usual Aswamedha sacrifice. This story is also followed up by the Śrīmad-Bhāgavata, which applies to him the epithets Adhirāṭ and Samrāṭ, *i.e.*, king of kings, and describes his subjugation of a number of races, tribes and kingdoms such as the Kirātas, the Hūṇas, the Yavaṇas, the

[1] III. 33.

[2] Panjikā VIII.: "एतेन ह वा ऐन्द्रेन महाभिषेकेन दीर्घतमा मामतेय: दौष्मन्तिं भरतं अभिषिषेच। तस्मात् उ दौष्मन्ति: भरत: समन्तं सर्व्वत: पृथिवीं जयन् परीयायाश्वेश्चंमेध्यैरीजे इत्यादि।"

Paundras and the like, and his ultimate renunciation of the world as an unreality in essence. Bharata, therefore, stood before the multitudinous peoples inhabiting the country that was called after him as the embodiment, the representative, of the dominant Aryan power which was fast accomplishing its work of colonising the whole country and bringing its different parts under the unifying discipline of a common culture and civilisation. Bhāratavarṣa is therefore another name for Aryanised India, the congenial fertile soil where Aryan culture planted itself and attained its fruition, the chosen abode which the pioneers of human civilisation adopted as the scene of their labours for the proper expression of their particular genius. And Bharata was held up as a convenient symbol, a comprehensible token of this early renaissance, of the conquest of a new thought and a new faith finding expression through their appropriate literature, disciplines and institutions, social, economic and political, of the accomplishment of a new cultural unity imposed upon and pervading a rich, manifold variety, round which were gathered, as in a system of federation, different creeds, cults and cultures with liberty to each to preserve its own special features and genius and contribute its own quota to enrich the central culture.[1]

[1] As pointed out by Prof. Benoy Kumar Sarkar, M.A., in his suggestive brochure on the *Pedagogy of the Hindus*, this synthetic and complex Indian culture was the result of the Indian system of education which adapted itself to national requirements in all ages, and he argues: "How otherwise can we account for the rise of the numerous Puranas, Sanhitas, and Tantras adapted to the needs of the people in different ages and provinces? . . . It was because of their mastery over the principles of Psychology and Sociology that the leaders of the community never neglected the superstitions, the mechanical rites and ceremonies, the diverse practices and usages and various religious customs and mythological notions obtaining in the country, but rather promoted the growth and development of a varied eschatology, a varied mythology and a varied religious system according to the varied geographical and historical condition of the people."

The idea of § V. is very well developed in Mr. B. C. Pal's *The Soul of India*.

VI

But besides this proof of a common name, there are other proofs to show that the fact of this fundamental unity of India was fully grasped by the popular mind in ancient times. Even such an old book as the *Ṛig-Veda*, one of the oldest literary records of humanity, reveals conscious and fervent attempts made by the Ṛiṣis, those profoundly wise organisers of Hindu polity and culture, to visualise the unity of their mother country, nay, to transfigure the mother earth into a living deity and enshrine her in the loving heart of the worshipper. This is best illustrated by the famous river-hymn[1] of the *Ṛig-Veda* where the various rivers of the Punjab, the perennial streams of plenty and good to which the country owes so much, which were at once the highways of commerce and culture alike, are deified by a grateful imagination and receive the

[1] *Rv*. X. 75.

nation's worship and homage. As the mind of the devotee contemplates in love and reverence those formative, beneficent agencies of nature contributing from time eternal to the making of his country, it naturally traverses the entire area of his native land and grasps an image of the whole as a visible unit and form. Certainly a better and simpler, a more convenient and significant formula could not be invented for the perception of the fatherland as one indivisible unit than the following prayer of the sloka in the aforesaid hymn:—

इमं मे गङ्गे यमुने सरस्वति
शुतुद्रि स्तोमं सचता परुष्ण्या ।
असिक्न्या मरुद्वृधे वितस्तयार्जीकीये
शृणुह्या सुषोमया ॥ [1]

[O ye Gangā, Yamunā, Sarasvati, Śatadru, and Paruṣñi, receive ye my prayers! O ye Marutbṛidhā, joined by the Asiknī, Vitastā, and Ārjikīyā joined by the Susomā, hear ye my prayers!]

[1] *Sutudri* = the Sutlej; *Paruṣñi* = the Ravi; *Asikni* = the Chenab; *Marudbṛidhā* = the combined course of the Akesines and Hydaspes (Roth); *Vitastā* = Gr. Hydaspes = Jheelum; *Ārjīkīyā* = the Vipas (according to Yāska) = the *Bias*; *Suṣomā* = the Indus (Yāska). See Map.

It calls up at once in the mind's eye a picture of the whole of Vedic India, and fulfils in a remarkable way the poet's purpose behind it of awakening the people's consciousness to the fundamental unity of their country. Nay, it does more: it elevates and refines patriotism itself into religion. To think of the mother country, to adore her as the visible giver of all good, becomes a religious duty; the fatherland is allotted its rightful place in the nation's daily prayers. The river-hymn[1] of the *Ṛig-Veda* therefore presents the first national conception of Indian unity, such as it was. It was necessarily conditioned by the geographical horizon

[1] The epithet *Sapta-sindhu*, the land of seven rivers, is applied to the whole of Vedic India in Ṛig. VIII., 24, 27, and is thus another expression of its geographical unity.

The *Epic* counterpart of the Vedic description of the Punjab is the following couplet of the *Mahābhārata*, Karṇa-parva, chapter 44:—

शतद्रुश्च विपाशा च तृतीयैरावती तथा।

चन्द्रभागा वितस्ता च सिन्धुः षष्ठा बहिर्गिरेः॥

attained in that age which seems to have been confined by the snowy mountains in the north, the Indus and the range of Suleiman mountains in the west, the Indus or the sea in the south, and the valley of the Jumna and the Ganges in the east. These limits practically include the whole of Northern India, the geographical unity of which was also recognised and suitably expressed in the designation of the entire territory by the common name of *Aryāvarta* in Vedic literature. Manu defines *Aryāvarta* as follows :—

> आसमुद्रात्तु वै पूर्व्वादासमुद्रात्तु पश्चिमात् ।
> तयोरेवान्तरं गिर्य्योरार्य्यावर्त्तं विदुर्बुधाः ॥—II. 21.

Medhātithi has the following commentary on the above: "पर्व्वतयोर्हिमवद्विन्ध्ययोर्यदन्तरं मध्यं सः आर्य्यावर्त्तो देशो बुधैः शिष्टैरुच्यते ।"

This explanation is quite in accord with that given by Amarakoṣa, viz. :—

> "आर्य्यावर्त्तः पुण्यभूमिः मध्यं विन्ध्यहिमालयोः ।"

So that Aryāvarta corresponds to the

territory between the Himalayas and the Vindhyas.[1]

VII

With the gradual extension of Aryan colonisation of India beyond the limits of the old Aryāvarta so as to embrace the whole of Dakshināpatha or Southern India, the old Vedic formula for the conception of Indian unity was supplemented by other appropriate formulae to give fitting expression to an expanding geographical consciousness. Thus the following Pauranic prayer is but an adaptation of the aforesaid river-hymn of the *Ṛig-Veda* to a new environment, to an expanded geographical horizon which embraced the whole of India within its limits:—

[1] The *Vasiṣṭha Dharma Sūtra* [i. 9], in accord with *Mānava Dharma Sūtra*, also defines Aryāvarta as the region between the Vindhya and the Himalaya, and these two ranges also seem to be the boundaries of the Aryan world in the *Kauṣītaki Upaniṣad* [ii. 13]. The *Bāla-rāmāyaṇa* of the poet Rajasekhara speaks of the river Narmadā as "the dividing line of *Aryāvarta* and *Dakṣiṇāpatha*."

गङ्गे च यमुने चैव गोदावरि सरस्वति ।
नर्मदे सिन्धुकावेरि जलेऽस्मिन् सन्निधिं कुरु ॥[1]

[O ye Gangā, Yamunā, Godavari, Sarasvati, Narmadā, Sindhu and Cauvery, come ye and enter into this water of my offering!]

This holy text for the sacrificial purification of water is daily repeated by millions of devout Hindus all over the continent during their baths and worships and cannot fail to lift them for the time being above the narrow cares, anxieties, and interests of domestic life to a higher, wider plane of thought, on which they feel something of the great "touch of nature which makes the whole world kin" and realise the vital, fundamental unity or kinship which binds them to a common fatherland, as members of the same nation-family. The same ennobling, elevating effect is produced on the national consciousness by the following popular

[1] We may compare in this connexion the mention of the *Sapta-Gangā* or the seven Gangās in *Śiva-purāṇa* [II. xiii.], viz., Gangā, Godāvari, Kāveri, Tāmraparṇi, Sindhu, Sarayu and Revā.

Pauranic couplet,[1] in which the whole of India is represented as the land of seven mountains, those chosen seats of contemplation and peace :—

महेन्द्रो मलयः सह्यः शुक्तिमानृक्षपर्व्वतः ।
विन्ध्यश्च पारियात्रश्च सप्तैते कुलपर्व्वताः ॥ [2]

Equally efficacious is the following text in enfranchising the mind from the limitations of a narrow, provincial, parochial outlook and opening it to a vision of the whole country of which all parts are equally sacred and entitled to homage :—

अयोध्या मथुरा माया काशी काञ्ची अवन्तिका ।
पुरी द्वारावती चैव सप्तैता मोक्षदायिकाः ॥ [3]

[1] It also occurs in the *Mahābhārata*, Bhīṣmaparva, ch. 9.

[2] *Mahendra* = the Mahendra Mali hills in Ganjam and the Eastern Ghats where Paraśurāma retired after his defeat by Rāma; *Malaya* = the southern part of the Western Ghats; *Sahya* = the northern part of the Western Ghats; *Rikṣa* = the eastern part of the Vindhyas, the mountains of Gondwana; *Pāripātra* or *Pāriyātra* = the western part of the Vindhyas, including the Aravalis. See Map.

[3] The seven sacred places named are: Ayodhyā, Mathurā, Māyā or Hardwar, Kāśi or Benares, Kāñchī or Conjeeveram, Avanti or Ujjani, and Dvārāvati or Dwarka in Guzerat.

Here India is represented as the land of seven principal sacred places which it is incumbent on every devotee to visit, and which cover between them practically the entire area of the country. It is also to be noted that the four most meritorious pilgrimages in India were placed by Saṅkarāchārya in the four extreme points of the country, so that the entire country may be known by the people and the whole area held sacred.[1] Saṅkarāchārya also established four *maṭhs* or monasteries in the four corners of India, viz., Jyotir-maṭh in the north, Sāradā-maṭh in the west, Sriṅgeri-maṭh in the south, and Govardhana-maṭh in the east. These were, as it were, the pillars of Saṅkara's religious victory (दिग्विजय), the capitals of his spiritual empire exercising its sway over the whole of India. The four traditional *tirthas* are similarly Svetagaṅgā

[1] These sacred places are Badari-Kedarnath in the north, Rāmesvara in the south, Dvārakā in the west and Jagannāth in the east.

in the east, Dhanustīrtha in the south, Gomatikuṇḍa in the west and Taptakuṇḍa in the north. There are similarly four traditional tanks (सरोवर), viz., Pampā, Vindu, Nārāyaṇa and Mānasa in the south, east, west and north respectively. There are, lastly, four popularly known *Kṣetras.* e.g., Mukti, Varāha, Harihara and Kuru. There are again recognised *three* principal temples for the worship of the sun in the east, north and west, viz., Konaraka (in Orissa), Multan [*Brahmapurāṇa*, I. 140, etc.], and Suryapura or Surat [*J.A.S.B.*, I. 387]. There are also similarly distinguished *eight* Vināyaka (Ganeśa) tirthas, viz., Moresvara, Ballāla, Lenādri, Siddhatek, Ojhar, Sthevara or Meura, Rāñjanagrāma and Mahaḍa.

The following passage, dear to every devout Hindu, enumerates the various places of Śaiva worship scattered throughout the whole of India :—

सौराष्ट्रे सोमनाथञ्च श्रीशैले मल्लिकार्जुनं ।
उज्जयिन्यां महाकालं ओंकारममरेश्वरे ॥

केदारं हिमवत्पृष्ठे डाकिन्यां भीमशङ्करम् ।
वाराणस्यां च विश्वेशं त्र्यम्बकं गौतमीतटे ॥
वैद्यनाथं चिताभूमौ नागेशं द्वारकावने ।
सेतुबन्धे च रामेशं घुश्मेशं च शिवालये ॥
एतानि ज्योतिर्लिङ्गानि सायं प्रातः पठेन्नरः ।
सप्तजन्मकृतं पापं स्मरणेन विनश्यति ॥[1]

A similar passage enumerates the principal sacred places consecrated to Viṣṇu which are daily repeated by millions of Hindus all over India.[2]

[1] The places may be thus identified: *Saurastra* = Gujrat; *Śrī-śaila* = the Palni hills in Madura; *Ujjain*; *Amaresvara* near Maṇḍalesvara and ancient Māhismati; the Himalayas (*Kedāranath*); *Dākinī* (unknown); *Benares*; *Gumti* or Godavari; *Chitābhūmi* = Baidyanath; *Setubandha* or Rāmesvara; *Śivālaya* (unknown).

[2] नारायणं बदर्याख्ये नैमिशे हरिमव्ययम् ।
शालग्रामं हरिक्षेत्रे अयोध्यायां रघूत्तमम् ॥ ४ ॥
मथुरायां बालकृष्णं मायायां मधुसूदनम् ।
काश्यांतु भोगशयनमवन्त्यामवनीपतिम् ॥ ५ ॥
द्वारवत्यां यादवेन्द्रं व्रजे गोपीजनप्रियम् ।
वृन्दावने नन्दसूनुं गोविन्दं कालियह्रदे ॥ ६ ॥
गोवर्धने गोपवेषं भवघ्नं भक्तवत्सलम् ।
रोमन्थपर्वते शौरिं हरिद्वारे जगत्पतिम् ॥ ७ ॥
प्रयागे माधवंचैव गयायांतु गदाधरम् ।

And in the story of Sati, the perfect wife, who can miss the significance of the fifty-two places in which fragments of the smitten body fell? "And one finger fell in Calcutta, and that is still the Kālighāt. And the tongue fell at Kangra (Jwālāmukhi) in the North Panjab and appears

---

गङ्गासागरगे विष्णुं चित्रकूटे तु राघवम् ॥ ८ ॥
नन्दिग्रामे राक्षसघ्नं प्रभासे विश्वरूपिणम् ।
श्रीकूर्मे कूर्ममचलं नीलाद्रौ पुरुषोत्तमम् ॥ ९ ॥
सिंहाचले महासिंहं गदिनं तुलसीवने ।
घृतशैले पापहरं श्वेताद्रौ सिंहरूपिणम् ॥ १० ॥
योगानन्दं धर्मपुर्यां काकुलेत्वाभ्रनायकम् ।
अहोबले गारुडाद्रौ हिरण्यासुरमर्दनम् ॥ ११ ॥
विठ्ठलं पांडुरंगे तु वेङ्कटाद्रौ रमासखम् ।
नारायणं यादवाद्रौ नृसिंहं घटिकाचले ॥ १२ ॥
वरदं वारणगिरौ काञ्चयां कमललोचनम् ।
यथोक्तकारिणं चैव परमेशपुराश्रयम् ॥ १३ ॥
पाण्डवानां तथा दूतं त्रिविक्रममथोन्नतम् ।
कामासिक्यां नृसिंहंच तथाष्टभुजसंज्ञकम् ॥ १४ ॥
मेघाकारं शुभाकारं शेषाकारंतु शोभनम् ।
अन्तरा शितिकण्ठस्य कामकोष्ठ्यां शुभप्रदम् ॥ १५ ॥
कालमेघं खगारूढं कोटिसूर्यसमप्रभम् ।

to this day, as licking tongues of fire, from underneath the ground. And the left hand fell at Benares which is for ever Annapūrnā, the Giver-of-Bread."[1] All the above passages, with their remarkable hold

[1] The *Devī-gītā* (eighth chapter) enumerates the various places throughout India sacred to the *Devī* or Durgā.

दिव्यं द्वीपप्रकाशंच देवानामधिपं मुने ॥ १६ ॥
प्रवालवर्णं द्वीपाभं काञ्चयामष्टादशस्थितम् ।
श्रीगृध्रसरसस्तीरे भान्तं विजयराघवम् ॥ १७ ॥
वीक्षारण्ये महापुण्ये शयानं वीरराघवम् ।
तोताद्रौ तुङ्गशयनं गजार्तिघ्नं गजस्थले ॥ १८ ॥
महाबलिं बलिपुरे भक्तिसारे जगत्पतिम् ।
महावराहं श्रीमुष्णे महीन्द्रे पद्मलोचनम् ॥ १९ ॥
श्रीरङ्गे तु जगन्नाथं श्रीधामे जानकीप्रियम् ।
सारक्षेत्रे सारनाथं खण्डने हरचापहम् ॥ २० ॥
श्रीनिवासस्थले पूर्णं सुवर्णं स्वर्णमन्दिरे ।
व्याघ्रपुर्यां महाविष्णुं भक्तिस्थाने तु भक्तिदम् ॥ २१ ॥
श्वेतह्रदे शान्तमूर्तिमग्निपुर्यां सुरप्रियम् ।
भर्गाख्यं भार्गवस्थाने वैकुण्ठाख्ये तु माधवम् ॥ २२ ॥
पुरुषोत्तमे भक्तसखं चक्रतीर्थे सुदर्शनम् ।
कुम्भकोणे चक्रपाणिं भूतस्थाने तु शार्ङ्गिणम् ॥ २३ ॥
कपिस्थले गजार्तिघ्नं गोविन्दं चित्रकूटके ।

on the heart of the people as texts of their daily prayers, give expression to a feeling for the fatherland, an absorbing passion for place which is hardly surpassed anywhere in the world, while a negative proof of the same emotion shows itself in the fact that all the holy and sacred places of the Indian lie within the limits

---

अनुत्तमं चोत्तमायां श्वेताद्रौ पद्मलोचनम् ॥ २४ ॥
पार्थस्थले परब्रह्म कृष्णकोट्यां मधुद्विषम् ।
नन्दपुर्यां महानन्दं वृद्धपुर्यां वृषाश्रयम् ॥ २५ ॥
असङ्गं सङ्गमग्रामे शरण्ये शरणं महत् ।
दक्षिणद्वारकायांतु गोपालं जगतां पतिम् ॥ २६ ॥
सिंहक्षेत्रे महासिंहं मल्लारिं मणिमण्डपे ।
निबिडे निबिडाकारं धानुष्के जगदीश्वरम् ॥ २७ ॥
मौकरे कालमेघंतु मधुरायांतु सुन्दरम् ।
वृषभाद्रौ महापुण्ये परमस्वामिसंज्ञकम् ॥ २८ ॥
श्रीमद्वरगुणे नाथं कुरुकायांरमासखम् ।
गोष्ठीपुरे गोष्ठीपतिं शयानं दर्भसंस्तरे ॥ २९ ॥
धन्वी मङ्गलके शौरिं बलाढ्यं भ्रमरस्थले ।
कुरङ्गेतु तथा पूर्णं कृष्णमेकं वटस्थले ॥ ३० ॥
अच्युतं क्षुद्रनद्यांतु पद्मनाभमनन्तके ।
एतानि विष्णोःस्थानानि पूजितानि महात्मभिः ॥ ३१ ॥

of India and not one of them in some far off Palestine.

VIII

This intense passion for fatherland, indeed, utters itself throughout Sanskrit literature. We select some of these references at random. The *Atharva Veda*, for instance, sings the praises of the mother country as the land of the brave and the pious, of heroism and enterprise, of commerce and trade, of science and art, of virtue and greatness, of countless medicinal herbs and plants;[1] the land, girt by the sea and fertilised by the sacred rivers like the Indus, and rich in grain and foodstuffs;[2] the land where our forefathers lived and worked, where the Asuras succumbed to the might of the

[1] *Av.* XII. 2—"नानावीर्या ओषधीर्या विभर्त्ति . . ."

[2] *Av.* XII. 3—"यस्यां समुद्र उत सिन्धुरापो यस्यामन्नं कृष्टयः संम्बभूवुः ।"

Devas;[1] the land which boasts of the highest mountain and the most beautiful forest;[2] the land of sacrificial rites and sacred pleasures, of valour and renown, of patriotism and self-sacrifice, of virtue and kindness.[3] There are passages also in other Sanskrit works which refer to India as the chosen land,[4] a veritable

[1] *Av.* XII. 5—"यस्यां पूर्व्वे पूर्व्वजना विचक्रिरे यस्यां देवा असुरानभ्यवर्त्तयन् ।"

[2] *Av.* XII. 11—"गिरयस्ते पर्वता हिमवन्तोऽरण्यं ते पृथिवि स्योनमस्तु ।"

[3] *Av.* XII. 1. 22—"भूम्यां देवेभ्यो ददति यज्ञं हव्यमरं-कृतम् ।"

Av. XII. 1. 41—

"यस्यां गायन्ति नृत्यन्ति भूम्यां मर्त्त्या व्यैलबाः ।
युध्यन्ते यस्यामाक्रन्दो यस्यां वदति दुन्दुभिः ॥"

[4] *Manu*, II. 17—"तं देवनिर्म्मितं देशं ब्रह्मावर्त्तं प्रचक्षते।"

Viṣṇu Purāṇa, II. iii. 24:—

गायन्ति देवाः किल गीतकानि
धन्यास्तु ते भारतभूमिभागे ।
स्वर्गापवर्गास्पदमार्गभूते
भवन्ति भूयः पुरुषाः सुरत्वात् ॥

heaven on earth, culminating in the great national utterance

"जननी जन्मभूमिश्च स्वर्गादपि गरीयसी"

('mother and motherland are higher than heaven itself').

IX

The same feeling for the fatherland has again spread over the whole continent a

---

[Thus do the gods sing the glories of Bhāratavarṣa: "More fortunate than we are they who are born in that land wherein lies the veritable road to heaven and salvation."]

Śrīmadbhāgavata, v. xix. 20, 27.

अहो बतैषां किमकारि शोभनम्
प्रसन्न एषां स्विदुत स्वयं हरिः ।
यैर्जन्म लब्धं नृषु भारताजिरे
मुकुन्दसेवौपयिकं स्पृहा हि नः ॥ २० ॥

*   *   *   *

यद्यत्र नः स्वर्गसुखावशेषितं
स्विष्टस्य सूक्तस्य कृतस्य शोभनम् ।
तेनाजनाभे स्मृतिमज्जन्म नः स्याद्-
वर्षे हरिर्यद्भजतां शं तनोति ॥ २७ ॥

network of shrines and sacred places which constitutes one of the distinguishing and differentiating features of India. For it goes without saying that the institution of pilgrimage is entirely an expression of love for the motherland, one of the modes of worship of the country which strengthens the religious sentiment and expands the geographical consciousness. Behind the religious merit and sanctity of pilgrimage there lies the admiration of place, of art, even of geographical significance. Benares in the North and Conjeeveram in the South are loved and visited because they are cathedral cities, rich in architecture, in treasure and in the associations of saints and scholars. We also feel that Jagannāth owes its position in no small degree to the sheer beauty of the sea and also perhaps to the cosmopolitanism of the place as the port through which long flowed the eastern trade. Allahabad, the Tirtharāja Prayāga, the prince of holy places, inevitably rose at the confluence of two mighty rivers mingling their waters. The perennial beauty of the Himalayas has captivated the national imagination and has made them the refuge of holy men, drawing unending streams of pilgrims. Indeed, the Hindu's pilgrimages are always to the glacier-clad mountain, the palm-clad sea-shore or ocean-isle, or the almost impenetrable depths of hill and jungle, where the tread of the generations of Man has scarcely been heard, and Nature left free to exercise her healing and healthful influence. Thus the Indian treats the beauty of place in a peculiar way, foreign to the West: his method of appreciating and celebrating it is quite different. A spot of beauty is no place for social enjoyment or self-indulgence; it is the place for self-restraint, for solitary meditation which leads the mind from nature up to Nature's God. Had Niagara been situated on the Ganges, how different would have been its valuation by humanity![1] Instead of occasional picnics and railway pleasure-trips, the perennial pilgrimage of worshipping crowds. Instead of parks, *asramas.* Instead of hotels, temples. Instead of ostentatious excess, simple austerity. Instead of the desire to harness its mighty forces to the chariot of human utility, an absorbing subjectivity, a complete detachment from the body and the outward world to feed the life of the spirit!

Thus the institution of pilgrimage is undeniably a most powerful instrument for developing the geographical sense in the people which enables them to think and feel that India is not a mere congeries of geographical fragments, but a single, though immense, organism, filled with the tide of one strong pulsating life from end to end. The visit to holy places as an imperative religious duty has made wide travelling a national habit

[1] Cf. Sister Nivedita's "*The Web of Indian Life,*" p. 241.

in India in all ages of life, with young and old alike, and travelling in ages preceding the era of steam and mechanical transport could not but promote a deep knowledge of the tracts traversed which is easily escaped by modern globe-trotters. It was this supremely Indian institution in fact which served in the past in place of the modern railway and facilities for travel to promote popular movements from place to place and intercommunication between parts producing a perception of the whole. It allowed no parochial, provincial sense to grow up which might interfere with the growth of the idea of the geographical unity of the mighty motherland; allowed no sense of physical comforts to stand in the way of the sacred duty of intimately knowing one's mother country; and softened the severities of old-world travelling by breaking the pilgrim's route by a holy halting place at short intervals.

It is difficult indeed to count up the

innumerable sacred spots which an overflowing religious feeling has planted throughout India. One of the best lists[1] of these is to be found in the Vanaparva

[1] The *Garuḍa-purāṇa* preserves some authentic lists of the Hindu holy places all over India. The following passage in the sixty-sixth chapter distinguishes the principal sacred places thus :—

शालग्रामोद्वारकाच नैमिषं पुष्करं गया।
वाराणसी प्रयागञ्च कुरुक्षेत्रञ्च सूकरं ॥
गङ्गा च नर्म्मदा गोदा चन्द्रभागा सरस्वती ।
श्रीक्षेत्रञ्च महाकालस्तीर्थान्येतानि शङ्कर ॥
सर्वं पापहराण्येव भुक्तिमुक्तिप्रदानिवै ।

But perhaps the best and a most exhaustive enumeration of holy places occurs in the eighty-first chapter, which passes in review the whole continent from the Himalayas to Cape Comorin in the following couplets :—

सर्वतीर्थानि वक्ष्यामि गङ्गातीर्थोत्तमोत्तमा ।
सर्वत्र सुलभागङ्गा त्रिषु स्थानेषु दुर्लभा ॥
हरिद्वारे प्रयागेच गङ्गासागरसङ्गमे ।
प्रयागं परमं तीर्थं मृतानां भुक्तिमुक्तिदम् ॥
सेवनात् क्षतपिण्डानां पापभित् कामदं नृणाम् ।
वाराणसी परं तीर्थं विश्वेशो यत्रकेशव: ॥
कुरुक्षेत्रं परं तीर्थं दानाद्भुक्तिमुक्तिदम् ।
प्रभासं परमं तीर्थं सोमनाथोऽस्ति यत्रच ॥
द्वारकाच पुरी रम्या भुक्तिमुक्तिप्रदायिका ।

of the Mahābhārata where two descriptions are given of the principal holy places, one by Nārada and the other by Dhaumya. Other such lists are to

---

प्राची सरस्वती पुण्या सप्तसारस्वतं परं ॥
केदारं सर्वपापघ्नं शम्भलग्राम उत्तमम् ।
नरनारायणं तीर्थं मुक्त्यै वदरिकाश्रमम् ॥
श्वेतद्वीपं पुरी माया नैमिषं पुष्करं परम्
अयोध्या चार्यतीर्थन्तु चित्रकूटश्च गोमतीम् ॥
वैनायकं महातीर्थं रामगिर्य्याश्रमं परम् ।
काञ्चीपुरी तुङ्गभद्रा श्रीशैलं सेतुवन्धनम् ॥
रामेश्वरं परं तीर्थं कार्त्तिकेयं तथोत्तमम् ।
भृगुतुङ्गं कामतीर्थं चामरकण्ठकं तथा ॥
उज्जयिन्यां महाकालः कुब्जके श्रीधरोहरिः ।
कुब्जायकं महातीर्थं कालसर्पिश्च कागदम् ॥
महाकेशीच कावेरी चन्द्रभागा विपाशया ।
एकाम्रञ्चतथा तीर्थं ब्रह्मेशं देवकोटकम् ॥
मथुराच पुरी रम्या शोणश्चैव महानदः ।
जम्बूसरो महातीर्थं तानि तीर्थानि विद्धिच ॥
सूर्यः शिवो गणो देवी हरिर्यत्रच तिष्ठति ।
एतेषुचतथान्येषु स्नानदानं जपस्तपः ॥
पूजाश्राद्धं पिण्डदानं सर्वंभवतिचाक्षयम् ।
शालग्रामं सर्वदं स्यात् तीर्थं पशुपतेः परम् ॥

be found in the various accounts of what are known as the Pīṭha-sthānas. The popularly known number, 52, is given by Tantra Chuḍāmani. According to Devī-

---

कोकामुखञ्च वाराहं भाण्डीरं स्वामिसंज्ञकम् ।
मोहदण्डेमहाविष्णुर्मन्दारे मधुसूदनः ॥
कामरूपं महातीर्थं कामाख्या यत्र तिष्ठति ।
पुण्ड्रवर्द्धनकं तीर्थं कार्त्तिकेयस्य यत्रच ॥
विरजन्त महातीर्थं तीर्थं श्रीपुरुषोत्तमम् ।
महेन्द्रपर्वतस्तीर्थं कावेरीच नदीपरा ॥
गोदावरी महातीर्थं पयोष्णी वरदा तथा ।
विन्ध्यः पापहरं तीर्थं नर्म्मदाभेद उत्तमः ॥
गोकर्णं परमं तीर्थं तीर्थं माहिष्मतीपुरी ।
कालञ्जरं महातीर्थं शुक्रतीर्थमनुत्तमम् ॥
कृतशौचं मुक्तिदञ्च शार्ङ्गधारीच दण्डके ।
विरजं सर्वदं तीर्थं स्वर्णाक्षं तीर्थनुत्तमम् ।
नन्दितीर्थं मुक्तिदञ्च कोटितीर्थफलप्रदम् ।
नासिक्यञ्च महातीर्थं गोवर्द्धनमतःपरम् ॥
कृष्णवेणी भीमरेखा गण्डकी याल्विरावती ।
तीर्थं विन्दुसरः पुण्यं विष्णुपादोदकं परम् ॥
श्रीरङ्गस्य हरे स्तीर्थं तापीश्रेष्ठा महानदी ।
सप्तगोदावरं तीर्थं तीर्थं कोणगिरिः परम् ॥
महालक्ष्मीर्यंच देवी प्रणीता परमा नदी ।

Bhāgavata, the number is 108 [7–30]. The Kubjikātantra also enumerates the various Siddhapithas throughout India. The Śiva-Charita distinguishes the Mahā-pīṭhas numbering 51 from the minor Upa-pīṭhas numbering 26. A reference to these holy places is also contained in the Kālika-purāṇa (chh. 18, 50, 61).

X

Along with this system and network of Hindu holy places should also be considered the multitude of monuments with which Buddhism and Jainism—ultimately and essentially but phases of Hindu thought—have adorned the land and influenced the geographical consciousness of large numbers of people

---

सह्याद्रौ देवदेवेश एकवीरः सुरेश्वरी ॥
गङ्गाद्वारे कुब्जावर्त्ते विन्ध्यके नीलपर्वते ।
स्नात्वा कनखले तीर्थे स भवेन्न पुनर्भवे ॥

under their direct sway. "Historically, both Buddhism and Jainism, may be regarded as offshoots or sects of Hinduism."[1] Buddhism in fact is the name given to Hinduism of the first few centuries of the Christian era, when precipitated in a foreign consciousness. Its special and most noteworthy contribution was a vast imperial organisation, highly centralised, coherent in all its parts, full of the geographical consciousness, uttering itself in similar architectural forms in the east and west of India, passionately eager to unify and elevate the people and to adorn the land. India became a self-contained, self-conscious unit, in full and living communication both by land and sea with China and Japan, Syria and Egypt, sending abroad ambassadors, merchants and missionaries with messages, commodities and ideas.

What the idea of pilgrimage is to the

[1] See V. A. Smith's "*A History of Fine Art in India*," etc., introduction.

Hindu mind, the worship of relics is to the Buddhist. The former realised itself in the planting of holy places, the latter in the erection of monuments beautifying the land. The Buddhist veneration of relics led to the construction of multitudes of domed cupolas (stupas, dagobās) for the safe custody of the relics, surrounded with accessory structures upon which were lavished all the resources of art; while the necessities of monastic life led to the erection of vihāras and chaityas, monasteries and churches, both rock-cut and structural. The *Pillars* (*lats*) at Delhi, Tirhut, Sankisa, Sanchi, etc.; the *chaitya-caves* and *viharas* at Bihar, Nasik, Ajanta, Elura, Karle, Kanheri, Bhaja, Bedsa, Dhamnar, Udaigiri, Bagh, etc.; *stupas* of Manikyala, Sarnath, Sanchi and Amaravati; the *gateways* and *stone railings* at Barahat (Bharhut), Mathura, Gaya, Sanchi and Amaravati; and lastly, the numerous Gandhara monasteries—all these, considering their widely-separated locations, point to the extensive area which was unified by a common artistic impulse, a single religious idea.

XI

We have now seen how the idea of the essential unity of the Indian world underlying its truly continental vastness and variety has seized the national consciousness and become one of its natural, integral contents. It is also clear that this particular consciousness could not be a sudden growth but required time for its development. Its evolution must naturally correspond at every stage to the evolution of geographical knowledge in the Indian mind. The perception of India as a single country must wait on an intimate geographical knowledge of the whole of India previously obtained.

It is therefore necessary to trace the development of this geographical knowledge and mark out its successive stages.

XII

It goes without saying that in the Vedic age the geographical horizon embraced only a part of India. The extent and limits of Vedic India may be inferred from the river-hymn and other geographical data in the *Ṛig-Veda.* Mention is made therein of some twenty-five streams, all but two or three of which belong to the Indus river system. The word *Sapta-Sindhavah* is once used to indicate Aryan India, the land of seven rivers, which are generally understood to mean the five rivers of the Punjab, together with the Indus and the Kabul, for which the Sarasvati was afterwards substituted. The easterly limit of the

Aryan home is indicated by the reference in one or two places to the rivers Jamunā and Ganges. Thus the widest geographical extent of Vedic India was the country bounded "by the snowy mountains in the north, the Indus and the range of the Suleiman mountains in the west, the Indus and the sea in the south, and the valley of the Yamuna and the Ganges in the east."[1] The country beyond the Vindhya range and the Narmadā river, which are not mentioned in the *Ṛig-Veda*, was not known to the Vedic Aryans.

Later Vedic literature does not show any knowledge of Southern India. The passage in the *Aitareya Brāhmaṇa* [vii. 18], in which Visvāmitra refers to the Andhras, Pundras, Sabaras, Pulindas and Mutibas as living on the borders of the Aryan settlements, only demonstrates that the Āryas were at that time acquainted with the whole country to the north of the

[1] Max Müller in *India: what can it teach us?* pp. 168, 174.

Vindhya and a portion to the south-east of that range.

XIII

The examination of the available evidence shows that the colonisation of Southern India did not accomplish itself till the seventh century B.C. Pāṇini, who "must have flourished in the beginning of the seventh century before the Christian era, if not earlier still,"[1] mentions many places and rivers which mostly belong to the Panjab and Afghanistan. The most southerly places mentioned by him are Kachchha [IV. 2, 133], Avanti [IV. 1, 176], Kosala [IV. 1, 171], Karusa[2] [IV. 1, 178], and Kalinga [IV. 1, 178].

The contemporary Pali literature points to the same conclusion. In one of the oldest Pali texts [the Sutta-Nipāta, 976) occurs the expression Dakkhinā-

[1] Sir R. G. Bhandarkar in his *Early History of the Deccan*.

[2] Eastern portion of Shahabad district in Behar.

patha,[1] which does not mean the whole of modern Dekkan, but only a remote settlement on the upper Godāvari. The expression does not occur in any one of the four Nikāyas. It occurs again in the later text [*Vin.* 1, 195, 196 ; 2, 298], but only to mean the same district near the Godāvari and in conjunction with Avanti. The Nikāyas refer to sea-voyages out of sight of land [see my *History of Indian Shipping*, Part I., ch. III.] and to Kaliṅga and Dantapura near the coast, while the *Vinaya* to Bharukaccha [3, 38] and the *Udāna* to Supparaka [1, 10]. The approximate geographical extent of the most ancient Buddhism (*i.e.*, about the time of Buddha) is stated *inter alia* in the *Mahāparinibbāna Sutta*, "where are named the

[1] Dakṣināpatha, lit., 'the path or road of the south; the southern road' was the technical expression for Southern India. The analogous expression for Northern India was Uttarapatha, lit., 'the path or road of the north, the northern road' which was of constant use, *e.g.*, in connection with Harṣavardhana of Kanouj, who is called 'समरसंसक्तसकलोत्तरपथेश्वरश्री-हर्षवर्द्धन,' the warlike lord of all the region of the North.

following chief towns as the dwelling-places of many nobles, Brahmans and Vaiśyas converted to Buddhism, viz., Champā, Rājagaha, Sāvatthi, Sāketa, Kosambī and Maga-Baranasi, comprising between them the kingdoms of Kāsi-Kosala and Magadha, together with the territories now known as Oudh and Bihar. The same geographical extent may be inferred from the distribution of Buddha's relics among eight places as mentioned in the *Mahāparinibbana Sutta* [S. B. E., Vol. XI., pp. 129 ff.], which are: Rājagaha, Vesālī, Kapilavathu, Allakappa, Rāmagāma, Vethadīpa, Pāvā, and Kusinārā, besides the shrines erected by Droṇa the Brahmin and the Moriyas of Pippalivana. The extent of the whole of old Buddhist India may be similarly inferred from passages in some Pāli books [e.g., *Aṅguttara*, 1. 213; 4. 252, 256, 260; *Vinaya Texts*, 2. 146], which enumerates the sixteen principal political divisions of the country as follows: (1) Aṅgā, (2) Magadhā, (3) Kāsī, (4) Kosalā, (5) Vajjī, (6) Mallā, (7) Cetī, (8) Vaṃsā, (9) Kurū, (10) Pañchālā, (11) Macchā, (12) Sūrasenā, (13) Assakā, (14) Avantī, (15) Gandhārā, and (16) Kambojā. Another similar list, indicating a slightly wider geographical extent, is to be found in the Govinda Sutta, 36 [*Dīgha-Nikāya*, XIX. 36], where the following seven provinces are distributed by the Brahman Govinda among King Renu and six other Kṣatriya princes, viz., (1) Kaliṅga, with its capital Dantapura; (2) Assaka, with its capital Potana; (3) Avanti, with its capital Māhismatī; (4) Sovira, with its capital Roruka; (5) Videha, with its capital Mithilā; (6) Aṅga, with its capital Champā; (7) Kāsi, with its capital Bārānasi.

The *Lalita-Vistara* [ch. III.] also mentions the existence of sixteen great States in the different countries of "Jambudvīpa," and also names the following places and dynasties in connection with a discussion of their fitness as the birthplace of the

Buddha, viz., (1) the *Vaideha* dynasty of *Magadha*; (2) the *Kosala* dynasty; (3) the *Vaṅsarāja* dynasty, of which the Tibetan name is *Vadsa*, with its capital Kauśambī; (4) the city state of *Vaiśalī*; (5) the *Pradyotana* dynasty which ruled in *Ujjayinī*; in the Chinese version it is called Mavanti, apparently a corruption of Avanti; (6) the city of *Mathurā*, where ruled the race of King Kaṅsa; (7) the city of *Hastināpura* of the Pāṇḍavas; (8) the city of *Mithilā*; (9) the country of the *Śakyas* with its capital Kapilavāstu, which was finally chosen as the fit birthplace for the Buddha. "He surveyed all the Kṣatriya royal dynasties in the continent named *Jambu* and found all of them tainted except the Sakya race, which was devoid of all defect."

Again, in the tenth chapter of the same work where the Bodhisattva names the 64 kinds of writing there is a reference to the following places and tribes: (1) Aṅgā, (2) Vaṅga, (3) Magadha, (4) the country of Śakāri, (5) Brahmavalli, (5) Dravida, (7) Dakṣiṇa, (8) Ugra, (9) Darada, (10) Khāsaya, (11) Chīna, (12) the country of Huna.

All the above references, Sanskrit as well as Pali, show that the geographical horizon of the Indians between the Vedic and early Buddhist periods did not embrace Southern India and Ceylon, the knowledge and colonisation of which belonged to a later period.

XIV

Southern India first floats into the Indian geographical horizon at least as early as the fourth century B.C. If the whole of India was unknown to Pāṇini, it was well-known to his commentator Kātyāyana, whom both popular tradition and modern scholarship assign to the time of the Nandas who preceded the Mauryas. Kātyāyana's reference to the derivatives

Pāṇḍyas, Cholas and Māhiṣmat, supplements in reality both the grammar and geography of Pāṇini.

There is also Greek evidence to show that the Indians had a very accurate knowledge of the form and extent of India in the time of Alexander's invasion. According to Strabo [*Geographia*, ii. 1, 6], Alexander "caused the whole country to be described by men well acquainted with it." This account was afterwards lent to Patrokles, the satrap under Seleukus Nikator and Antiochus Soter, and was accepted as true by Eratosthenes and Strabo who on the basis of that account have given certain distances and dimensions about India which approximate to their modern measurements.

We also know from history how wide and deep was the geographical knowledge of the whole of India under the Maurya Emperor. Thus the *Arthaśāstra* of Kauṭilya, which is generally attributed to Chānakya, the minister of Chandragupta, shows a good knowledge of the economic products of the various parts of India including the south. The trade-routes of India are divided broadly into two classes:[1] (1) the Northern, *i.e.*, those leading to the Himalayas and called Haimavatah; (2) the Southern called Dakṣiṇāpathah. Of these the former are noted for their access to such commodities as elephants, horses, perfumes, skins, silver and gold, while the latter convey such valuable things as conch-shells, diamond, precious stones, pearls and gold, of which the Tamil land is the famous and fertile source. Commercially the latter are therefore held to be more important than the former. Southern India is also recognised to be abounding in mines. Some of the rivers of Southern

[1] "हैमवतो दक्षिणापथाच्छ्रेयान् हस्त्यश्वगन्धदन्ताजिनरूप्यसुवर्णपण्याः सारवत्तरा इत्याचार्याः ।
नेति कौटिल्यः—कम्बलाजिनाश्वपण्यवर्जाः शङ्खवज्रमणिमुक्तासुवर्णपण्याश्च प्रभूततराः दक्षिणापथे ।
दक्षिणापथेऽपि बहुखनिः . . ." Bk. VII. ch. 12.

India and of Ceylon are mentioned as sources of pearls, *e.g.*, Tāmraparṇīka, Kula, Chūrṇa; and also some mountains, *e.g.*, Pāndyavātaka, Mahendra. In the extreme north, some Himalayan villages are mentioned as the source of skins, *e.g.*, Viśī, Mahāviśī, Aroha, Bahlava and also Nepal as sources of blankets. Kāmbhoja (Afghanistan, the *Kaofu* of Hiuen Tsang), Sindhu (Sindh) and Āratta (Panjab, lit. land of the kingless) are also mentioned as sources of the supply of horses. Among eastern countries are mentioned Vaṅga, Pauṇḍra, Suvarṇa-Kudyaka (probably Kāmarūpa, as suggested by the commentator), Magadha, Kāśī and Kaliṅga, which were noted even in those early days for their cotton and silk fabrics. Aṅga, Karūṣa, Prāchya and Kaliṅga are also mentioned as sources of the supply of elephants. Mādura in the south, Aparānta on the west, Māhiṣa in the Deccan are also mentioned for their cotton fabrics. Surāstra is also mentioned for its supply of elephants and Sauvira for horses. Lastly, some countries outside India are also mentioned with which she had trade across the seas (Pārasamudraka), *e.g.*, Svarṇabhūmi noted for its perfumes, China for its silks (Chīnapaṭṭāḥ) and Arabia (Vanāyu) for its horses.[1]

The Edicts of Asoka also supply convincing evidence that the whole of India was known in his days. The southern independent kingdoms, such as the Chola, Pandya, Satiyaputra and Keralaputra, are mentioned, together with the Andhras and Pulindas. There are also mentioned the border nations on the north-west, west and the Deccan such as the Yonas, Kambojas, Gandharas, Rashtrikas, Pitenikas (probably connected with Paithan), Nabhatas. The conversion of Ceylon by Mahendra may also be taken to be a historical fact, supported as it is by both northern and southern tradition.

Thus by the time of the Maurya

[1] See *Arthaśāstra*, pp. 50, 75—81. Mysore Ed.

Empire the knowledge of all parts of India was a common possession, a content of the popular geographical consciousness. And we accordingly find the contemporary and subsequent literature replete with geographical details.

XV

Patañjali (150 B.C.) shows considerable advance upon Kātyāyana and has intimate knowledge of the south. Besides mentioning Māhiṣmatī [Mahābhaṣya on Pān. III. 1, 26], Vaidarbha [IV. 1, 4], Kānchipura [IV. 2, 2] and Kerala or Malabar [IV. 1, 175] he notices some lingual usages in the south [I. 1, 19].[1]

It is difficult to ascertain the precise chronological value of the great epics Rāmāyaṇa and Mahābhārata as we have them now. Popular Hindu belief assigns

[1] अस्ति च लोके सरसीशब्दस्य प्रवृत्तिः दक्षिणापथेहि महान्ति सरांसि सरस्य इत्युच्यते

to the Rāmāyaṇa[1] an earlier date and is supported by the fact that it shows a much less knowledge of Southern India than the Mahābhārata. Among the places lying to the south are mentioned Utkala, Kaliṅga, Dasārna [Bhilsa], Avanti and Vidarbha, which do not carry us very far beyond the line of the Vindhyas. Between these and the southernmost countries of the Cholas, Pāndyas and Keralas the Rāmāyaṇa mentions no other place but Daṇḍakāraṇya. This state of geographical knowledge carries us back to the days of later Vedic literature before the 7th century B.C. Sugriva's descriptions, however, of places and peoples in the Kiṣkindhā Kāṇḍa [Sargas 40–43] exhibit broadly the conception of India as a whole which is distinguished from parts forming what may be termed Greater India, as also from surrounding countries and nations.

[1] The *Arthaśāstra* refers to the story of the *Rāmāyaṇa* and *Mahābhārata* thus: "मानात् रावणः परदाराना-प्रयच्छन् दुर्योधनो राज्यादंशं च।" [Mysore ed., p. 11.]

That a Mahābhārata existed before Pāṇini is proved by his allusions to Vāsudeva, Arjuna and Yudhiṣṭhira. The geographical horizon of the Epic as we have it now is indicated in the passage, among others, where Sahadeva is represented to have subdued the Pāṇḍyas, Dravidas, Udras, Keralas and Andhras [Sabhāp. ch. 31]. It is also indicated in the passage [Bhīṣmap. ch. 9], which enumerates the seven principal mountains of India and also by the list of some 200 rivers given in the tenth chapter of Bhīṣmaparva, where are mentioned the southerly rivers, Mahānadī, Godāvarī, Kriṣṇā and Kāverī, Narmadā, Kriṣṇavēnī, Vēna, Tunga-Vēna. The Bhīṣmaparva, chapter IX., mentions 157 peoples belonging to Northern India and 50 peoples belonging to the south of the Narmadā. The Vanaparva, as has been already stated, affords interesting geographical data in the lists of holy places it gives. The holy places in the south mentioned are the Godāvarī, Vēna, Payoṣṇī, the Agastya-tīrtha and the Varuṇa-tīrtha, the Tāmraparṇī and Gokarṇa-tīrtha, the Kavērī and the Kanyā-tīrtha (probably Kanyā Kumāṛi, Cape Comorin). The itinerary of the Pāṇḍavas is also similarly interesting. It refers to such places as the Vaitaraṇī in Kaliṅga, the Mahēndra mountain where lived Paraśurāma, and the Pāṇḍya country whence they reached Surpāraka.

Besides this intimate knowledge of the parts, the Mahābhārata presents a conception of the whole of India as a geographical unit in the famous passage in the Bhīṣmaparva where the shape of India is described as an equilateral triangle, divided into four smaller equal triangles, the apex of which is Cape Comorin and the base formed by the line of the Himalaya mountains. As remarked by Cunningham [*Ancient Geography of India*, p. 5], "the shape corresponds very well with the general form of the country, if we extend the limits of India to Ghazni on the north-west and fix the other two points of the triangle at Cape Comorin and Sadiya in Assam."

XVI

The geographical knowledge of the Mahābhārata is followed up by all the Purāṇas, which are well-known for their detailed information regarding the places and peoples of India. They also present the conception of India as a geographical unit in their description of the country as made up of nine divisions, viz., Indra, Kasērumat, Tāmraparṇa, Gabhastimat, Kumarikā, Nāga, Saumya, Varuna, Gāndharva, which agree with those of the famous astronomer Bhāskarāchārya [Siddhāntaśiromaṇi, ch. III., 41].

Varāhamihira [Vṛihat - Saṅhitā, ch. XIV.], however, gives a different list of the Nine Divisions which deserves a more than passing notice for the wealth of topographical details it presents. It may be given as follows:—

I. Central Division: Tribes—Kurus, Pañchālas, Pāṇḍus, Sūrasenas, Vatsas, etc. Towns—Mathurā, Sāketa. Rivers —Yamunā and Sarasvatī.

II. Eastern Division: Tribes—Ambasṭhas, Kauśalakas, Pauṇḍras, Prāgjyotiṣas, Tāmraliptikas and Utkalas. Countries—Kośala, Mithilā, Kāśī, Magadha, Puṇḍra, Tāmalipti, Samatata, Udra, etc.

III. South-eastern Division: Tribes — Chedikas, Dasārṇas, Niṣādas, etc. Countries — Aṅga (Chedi), Upavaṅga, Vaṅga, Kaliṅga, Andhra, Vidarbha, etc. Mountains—the Vindyas.

IV. South Division: Tribes—Ābhiras, Āvantakas, Cheryas, Kairalakas, etc., mariners (वारिचर), etc. Countries — Avanti's beryl-mines (Vaidūrya), Bhārukachchha, Chitrakūṭa, places for obtaining conch-shells, Kāñchī, Laṅkā, southern ocean, places for obtaining pearls, Siṅhala,

Talikata, Vellura, Chera, Chola, Kachchha, Karṇāṭa, Kerala, Koṅkana, etc. Forests —Daṇḍakavana. Mountains—Dardura, Kusuma, Mahendra, Malaya, Malindya, Riṣyamūka, Sūrpa, etc. Rivers—Kavērī, Kṛiṣṇā, Tāmraparṇī and Vēnā.

V. South-west Division: Tribes — Ābhiras, Aravas, Barbaras, Kirātas, Mākaras, Pahlavas, Sindhus, Sauviras, Sudras, Yavanas, etc. Countries—Mahārṇava, Ānarta, Drāviḍa, Kambhōja, Pārasava, Surāsṭra, etc.

VI. Western Division: Tribes—Aparāntakas, Haihayas, Mlechchhas, Śakas, Vaiśyas, etc.

VII. North-west Division: includes Hārahauras, Stri-rājya, and the river Veṇumatī.

VIII. Northern Division: Tribes—Huṇas, Kaikayas, Udīchyas, etc. Towns — Puṣkalāvatī, Takṣaśilā. Countries — Gāndhāra, Uttarakuru. Mountains — Dhanuṣmat, Himavat, Kailāsa, etc. River—Yamunā.

IX. North-east Division: includes Kāśmīra.

XVII

We may conclude the above account of the development of Indian geographical knowledge by a reference to the geography of Kālidāsa. In the conquests of Raghu are mentioned (in the east), the Suhmas, the Vaṅgas, the river Kapiśā, the Utkalas, the Kalingas with the mountain Mahendra; in the south, the river Kāverī and, beyond it, the Pāṇḍyas with their pearls produced at the mouth of the Tāmraparṇī, the mountains Malaya and Dardura, and, crossing them, the Keralas; on the west, crossing the Muralā river, Aparānta between the Sahya range and the sea, the Pārasikas; in the north, the Yavanas, the Hūṇas, the Kambōjas, the Kirātas and other hilly tribes near the Kailāsa mountain; Prāgjyotiṣa in the extreme east. In the Meghadūta the places mentioned on the route of the cloud messenger from Rāmagiri to Alakā are the following: Sātpura hills, Mālava, the Revā (Narmadā), Vindhya range, Dasārṇa, capital Vidiśā, Ujjayinī on the Śiprā, river Gandhavatī, Gambhīrā, Devagiri, Charmaṇvatī, Daśapura, Kurukṣetra, the Sarasvatī, the Kankhala hill near the Ganges, the source of the Ganges, Mount Kailāsa, Mānasa lake and Alakā.

XVIII

We have now seen how the Indians in ancient times before the era of steam and mechanical locomotion possessed a thorough knowledge of the different parts, tribes and races of India welded together into a whole which was so essential to their realisation of the idea of the geographical unity of their vast country. We have also seen that it was not a mere intellectual conception or an abstract idea but a vivid realisation through the heart; not the happy hit of a momentary inspiration but the settled habit of national thought induced by religious texts and daily prayers.

But along with the influence of religion as explained above, there was also the influence of *politics* in producing this popular consciousness of Indian geographical unity. History records the names of many Indian rulers who succeeded in realising their ambition of establishing a suzerainty over the whole of India which was accordingly thought of and used as a unit, as the common field of national activity. Such a ruler in older days was Harṣavardhana, who reigned from 606 to 648 A.D. over an empire that embraced the whole of the basin of the Ganges (including Nepal) from the Himālayas to the Narmada, besides Malwa, Gujrat and Surāṣṭra, and won for itself recognition as a paramount power in the land. Such a ruler, too, in yet older days was Samudra Gupta in the fourth century, A.D., who carried his victorious arms from the Ganges to the border of the Tamil country and thus achieved the political unification of a large part of India with an alliance extending from the Oxus to Ceylon. Such a ruler again in the past before the Christian era was Asoka the Great, one of the most illustrious in the illustrious roll of Indian Emperors, whose empire extended over the entire territory stretching from Afghanistan to Mysore, being "far more extensive than British India of to-day, including Burma" (V. A. Smith's *Asoka*, p. 81), and became a self-conscious political power with active international relations. And such a ruler was also Chandragupta, wrongly supposed to be the first historical paramount Sovereign of India, under whom also India realised herself as a political unit as she was already by nature a geographical unit.

XIX

It is a mistake to suppose that Chaṇdragupta was the first to introduce to Indian politics this conception of a single power dominating the whole country, for the idea was certainly much older than Chandragupta and was handed down from remote antiquity. The conception of a Chakravarti Raja or suzerain receiving the tribute and allegiance of subordinate kings has been one of the most familiar political notions of the ancient Hindus. Vedic literature furnishes a crop of terms for a paramount sovereign. These are :—

(1) *Adhirāja*, which occurs fairly often throughout the early literature to denote overlord among kings or princes. Thus it is found in the *Ṛig-Veda*, X. 128, 9; *Atharvaveda*, VI. 98, 1 and IX. 10, 24;

Taittiriya Sañhitā, II. 4, 14, 2; *Maitrāyani Sañhitā*, IV. 12, 3; *Kāṭhaka Sañhitā*, VIII. 17; *Taittiriya Brāhmaṇa*, III. 1, 2, 9 (*adhirājan*); *Śatapatha Brāhmaṇa*, V, 4, 2, 2; *Nirukta*, VIII. 2.

(2) *Rājādhirāja*, King of Kings, which is found in the later *Taittiriya Āranyaka*, I. 31, 6.

(3) *Samrāj*, which is used to mean superior ruler, sovereign, expressing a greater degree of power than king. It occurs in the *Ṛig-Veda*, III. 55, 7; 56, 5; IV. 21, 1; VI. 27, 8; VIII. 19, 32; also in the *Vājasaneyī Sañhitā*, V. 32; XIII. 35; XX, 5, etc.; also in the *Śatapatha Brāhmaṇa*, V. 1, 1, 13 [cf. XII. 8, 3, 4; XIV. 1, 3, 8], where the *Samrāj* is asserted to have a higher authority and rank than a king, and to have become one by the sacrifice of the *Vājapeya*. The epithet is also applied to Janaka of Videha in *Śatapatha Brāhamṇa*, XI. 3, 2, 1. 6; 2, 2, 3; and in *Bṛihadāranyaka Upanisad*, IV. 1, 1; 3, 1. It is applied in the

Aitareya Brāhmaṇa, VIII. 14, 2, 3, as the title of the Eastern kings, the kings of the Prāchyas (suggestive of Magadhan imperialism). The title for the Southerners, the kings of the people called *Sattvats*, is *Bhoja*; that for the Western kings, the kings of the peoples called *Nīchyas* and *Apāchyas*, is *Svarāṭ*; that for the kings of the North, beyond the Himalayas, viz., the countries Uttara Kuru and Uttara-Madra, is *Virāṭ*; and that for the kings of the middle country, viz., of the Kuru-Pañchālas and Usinaras, is simply Rāja.[1]

[1] "साम्राज्याय तास्मादेतस्यां प्राच्यां दिशि ये के च प्राच्यानां राजानः साम्राज्यायैव तेऽभिषिच्यन्ते ।

तस्मादेतस्यां दक्षिणस्यां दिशि ये के च सत्वतां राजानो भौज्यायैव ते अभिषिच्यन्ते ।

तस्मादेतस्यां प्रतीच्यां दिशि ये के च नीच्यानां राजानो येऽपाच्यानां स्वाराज्यायैव ते अभिषिच्यन्ते ।

तस्मादेतस्यामुदीच्यां दिशि ये के च परेण हिमवन्तं जनपदा उत्तरकुरव उत्तरमद्रा इति वैराज्यायैव तेऽभिषिच्यन्ते ।

तस्मादस्यां ध्रुवायां मध्यमायां प्रतिष्ठायां दिशि ये के च

(4) *Ekarāja*: meaning "sole ruler," "monarch." It is used metaphorically in the *Ṛig-Veda*,[1] VIII. 37, 3, but in the literal sense in the *Aitareya Brāhmaṇa*,[2] VIII. 15, as well as in the *Atharvaveda*,[3] III. 1, 4, 1.

According to *Śukranīti* [I. 183–187, ed. Oppert], the generic term *Nṛipati* (नृपति) embraces the following classes of kings arranged in an ascending scale of income and power, viz., Sāmanta (सामन्त), Māṇ-

---

कुरुपञ्चालानां राजानः सवशोशीनराणां राज्यायैव तेऽभिषिच्यन्ते राजेत्येनानभिषिक्तानाचक्षते ॥"

[1] "एकराळस्य भुवनस्य राजसि शचीपत इन्द्र विश्वाभिरूतिभिः ।"

[2] ". . . पृथिव्यै समुद्र पर्य्यन्ताया एकराड़िति ।"

[3] "आ त्वागन् राष्ट्रं सह वर्चसोदिहि प्राङ् विशांपतिरेकराट्त्वं विराज," which is thus paraphrased by *Sāyana*: हे राजन् त्वां राष्ट्रं शत्रुभिराक्रान्तं स्वकीयं राज्यं पुनरागमत ततस्त्वं वर्चसा बलेन सह उदिहि उदितः प्रख्यातो भव । अनन्तरं प्राक् पूर्वं विशां प्रजानां सर्वासां पतिः पालकः सन् एकराट् निःसपत्नो मुख्यो राजा भूत्वा त्वं विराज विशेषेण दीप्यस्व ॥

dalika (माण्डलिक), Rājā (राजा), Mahārāja (महाराजा), Samrāṭ (सम्राट्), Virāṭ (विराट्), and Sārvabhauma (सार्व्वभौम).

XX

Along with these terms for the suzerain there were also corresponding terms to indicate paramount power, sovereignty or overlordship. Thus the term *Rājya* is the general word denoting "sovereign power." It occurs in *Atharvaveda*, III. 4, 2; IV. 8, 1; XI. 6, 15; XII. 3, 31; XVIII. 4, 31. It also occurs in *Taittiriya Saṅhitā*, II. 1, 3, 4; 6, 6, 5; VII. 5, 8, 3, etc.; in *Aitareya Brāhmaṇa*, VII. 23, etc., and *Jaiminīya Upaniṣad Brāhmaṇa*, I. 4, 5. In some places the word *Svārājya*,[1]

[1] Might it not refer to republics or free states such, for instance, as those of the Licchavis, the Sakyas, the Mallas of Kusinara which were themselves also called by the name of Rājya (राज्य) with their Presidents called Rājā (राजा)? Thus according to the *Arthaśāstra* [xi. i, 160–161] the title *Rājā* applies to the heads of the common-

"uncontrolled dominion," is opposed to Rājya: *e.g.*, *Kāthaka Saṅhitā*, XIV. 5; *Maitrāyaṇi Saṅhitā*, I. 11, 5 (cf. *Taittiriya Brāhmaṇa*, I. 3, 2, 2). The *Aitareya Brāhmaṇa* [VIII. 12, 4, 5, etc.] gives a whole series of terms to indicate various shades and degrees of sovereignty, viz.:—*Rājya*, *Sāmrājya*, *Bhaujya*, *Svārājya*, *Vairājya*, *Pāramasthya*, *Māhārājya*, *Ādhipatya*, *Svāvaśya*. The term *Ādhipatya* also occurs in *Pañchaviṅsa Brāhmaṇa*, XV. 3, 35, and in *Chhāndogya Upaniṣad*, V. 2, 6.[1]

---

wealths of Lichchhivika, Vṛijika, Mallaka, Madraka, Kukura, Kuru, Pāñchāla, etc. ("लिच्छिविकवृजिक-मल्लक-मद्रक-कुकुर-कुरु-पाञ्चालादयो राजशब्दोपजीविनः।")

What lends colour to the supposition is the reference in the *Aitareya Brāhmana* to the kings of the Western peoples who were called *Svarāṭ* as distinguished from the Eastern kings known as the *Samrāts*. For the free states and clans of ancient India, see Rhys David's *Buddhist India*, p. 174.

[1] Among other terms preserved in Sanskrit literature to indicate paramount sovereignty are:—*Sārvabhauma* (सार्व्वभौम), *Rājarāja* (राजराज), *Visvarāt* (विश्वराट्), *Chakravarttī* (चक्रवर्त्ती), etc.

XXI

Next there were the well-known ceremonies[1] in connection with the coronations of emperors. These were generally the Vājapeya and the Rājasūya, the accounts of which as preserved in Vedic literature demonstrate how firmly the conception of an Ekarāt (one-sovereign) India seized the popular mind. According to the *Śatapatha Brāhmaṇa* [V. 1, 1, 13] and also *Kātyāyana Śrauta Sutra* [XV. 1, 1, 2], the Vājapeya is the superior sacrifice because it bestows on the sacrificer paramount sovereignty (Sāmrājya), while the Rājasūya merely confers royal dignity (Rājya). In the words of the above-

[1] An interesting and informing article on "Rituals at Hindu Coronation: its Constitutional Aspects," by Mr. Kashiprasad Jayaswal, B.A. (Oxon), Bar.-at-Law, appeared in the *Modern Review* for January, 1912.

mentioned verse of the *Śatapatha Brāhmaṇa*, "by offering the Rājasūya he becomes king, and by the Vājapeya (he becomes) emperor (Samrāj); and the office of king is the lower and that of emperor the higher; a king might indeed wish to become emperor, for the office of king is the lower and that of emperor the higher; but the emperors would not wish to become kings, for the office of king is the lower and that of emperor the higher."[1] According, however, to other authorities, the Vājapeya is the preliminary ceremony performed by a king who is elected paramount sovereign by a number of petty rājās, this sacrifice being followed in due course by the installation and consecration ceremony, the Rājasūya. Thus, as laid down in *Āsvalāyana Śrauta Sūtra* [IX. 9, 19], "after performing the

[1] "राजा वै राजसूयेनेष्ट्वा भवति। सम्राड् वाजपेयेनावरं हि राज्यं परं साम्राज्यं कामयेत वै राजा सम्राड् भवितुमवरं हि राज्यं परं साम्राज्यम।"

Vājapeya a king may perform the Rājasūya." With this rule would seem to accord the relative values assigned to the two ceremonies in the *Taittiriya Saṅhitā* [V. 6, 2, 1] and the *Taittiriya Brāhmaṇa* [II. 7, 6, 1], according to which the Vājapeya is a Samrātsavā or consecration to the dignity of a paramount sovereign, while the Rājasūya is called a "Varunasavā," *i.e.*, according to Sāyaṇa, a consecration to the universal sway wielded by Varuna (cf. *Sāṅkhyāyana Śrauta Sūtra*, XV. 13, 4: "for it is Varuna whom they consecrate"). In much the same sense also we have doubtless to understand the rule in which Lātyāyana defines the object of the Vājapeya [VIII. 11, 1], viz., "Whomsoever the Brahmans and kings (or nobles) may place at their head, let him perform the Vājapeya."[1] Among the rites peculiar to the Vājapeya, the most

[1] "यं ब्राह्मणा राजानश्च पुरस्कुर्वीरन् स वाजपेयेन यजेत ।"

interesting is the chariot race, in which the sacrificer is allowed to carry off the palm, and from which the sacrifice derives its name. After the chariot race the next interesting item is the mounting of the sacrificial post by the sacrificer (the king-elect) and his wife, from which homage is made to the mother Earth, followed by the seating on the throne, the symbol of sovereignty, "for he gains a seat above others" [*Śatapatha Brāhmaṇa*, V. 2, 1, 24]. The ascent to the throne as a symbol of kingship is also mentioned in the *Atharvaveda* [III. 1, 4, 2], where the throne is most felicitously described as the highest point in the body politic ("rāstrasya kakudi śrayasva"). The sacrificer is then duly proclaimed King[1]: "All ruler is he, N. N.! All ruler is he, N. N.!" [*Śatapatha Brāhmaṇa*, V. 2, 2, 15]. And also in the following

[1] "सघाडयमसौ सघाडयमसाविति निवेदितमेवैनमेतत् सन्तम ।"

words[1]: "Thine is this state, thou art the ruler, the ruling lord—thou art firm and steadfast—to thee the state is given for agriculture, for well-being, for wealth, for prosperity, *i.e.*, for the welfare of the people, the common weal" [*ibid.* V. 2, 1, 25].

XXII

The Rājasūya, or inauguration of a king, was a more complex ceremony, which consisted of a long succession of sacrificial performances spread over a period of upwards of two years. It is referred to in the *Atharvaveda* [IV. 8, 1; XI. 7, 7] and later literature such as *Taittiriya Saṅhitā* [V. 6, 2, 1], *Aitareya*

[1] "इयं ते राडिति राज्यमेवास्मिन्नेतद् दधात्यथैनमासादयति यन्तासि यमन इति यन्तारमेवैनमेतद् यमनमासां प्रजानां करोति ध्रुवोऽसि धरुण इति ध्रुवमेवैनमेतद् धरुणमस्मिंल्लोके करोति कृष्यै त्वा क्षेमाय त्वा रय्यै त्वा पोषाय त्वेति साधवे त्वेत्येवैतदाह ।"

Brāhmaṇa [V. 1, 1, 12], etc. The rite is described at great length in the Sutras, but its main features are clearly outlined in the Brāhmanas, especially in the *Śatapatha*, and also in *Maitrāyaṇī Saṅhitā* [IV. 3, 1, etc.], *Taittiriya Saṅhitā* [I. 8, 1, 1, etc.], while the verses used in the ceremony are preserved in the Saṅhitās of the Yajurveda, *e.g.*, *Taittiriya Saṅhitā* [I. 8], *Kāthaka Saṅhitā* [XV.], *Maitrāyaṇī Saṅhitā* [II. 6], and *Vājasaneyī Saṅhitā* [X.].

One of the most interesting features of the Rājasūya is the ceremony of the Ratnahavīṅṣi or jewel offerings. The recipients of these offerings, the *ratninah*, were all the essential officers of the state representing its principal departments: they are, metaphorically, the "jewels" in the crown of sovereignty. They are mentioned in the *Śatapatha Brāhmaṇa* [V. 3, 1, 3, etc.] in the following order: (1) Commander-in-chief (senanī); (2) the king's court chaplain (पुरोहित); (3) the queen (महिषी); (4) the court-minstrel and chronicler (सूत); (5) the head of the village community (ग्रामणी); (6) the chamberlain (क्षत्तृ); (7) the head of the treasury (संग्रहीतृ), which is explained by Sāyana as धनसंग्रहकर्ता कोशाध्यक्ष; (8) the collector of taxes and revenue (भागदुघ); (9) the superintendent of dicing (अक्षावाप); (10) the superintendent of games and forests (गो-विकर्तन), who, according to Sāyana, was the constant companion of the king in the chase; and (11) the courier (पालागल). There is another list given in the *Taittiriya Sañhitā* [I. 8, 9, 1, etc.] and *Brāhmaṇa* [I. 7, 3, 1, etc.] which omits Go-nikartana and the courier and includes Rājanya. Likewise the *Maitrāyanī Sañhitā* [II. 6, 5; IV. 3, 8] mentions Rājan, Vaisyagrāmanī and Takṣa-ratha-kārau,[1]

[1] The Ratha-kāra, chariot-maker, is mentioned in the *Atharvaveda* [iii. 5, 6] as one of those who are to be subjects to the king, and seems to be regarded generally as a representative of the industrial population. He is also referred to in the Yajurveda Sañhitās [*e.g.*; *Kāthak*, xvii. 13; *Maitrāyanī*, ii. 9, 5; *Vājasaneyī*, xvi. 17; xxx. 6] and in the Brahmanas [*e.g.*, *Taittiriya*, i. 1, 4, 8; iii. 4, 2, 1; *Śatapatha*, xiii. 4, 2, 17], and in all these passages he seems to be of a formed caste.

i.e., the carpenter and chariot-maker (probably the representatives of industry). The *Kāthaka Saṅhitā* [XVI. 4] also gives the same list, but substitutes Go-vyacha and omits Takṣa-ratha-kārau.

These lists were a development out of the simpler list given in the *Atharva-veda* [III. 5, 7] of the Rāja-kartṛis or Rāja-kṛits who, not themselves kings, aided in the consecration of the king. These were the Sūta, charioteer, the grāmaṇī, the village chief, and the people.[1] The word Rāja-kartā in the *Aitareya Brāhmaṇa* [VIII. 17, 5] is explained by the commentator to mean the king's father, brother, etc. It is, however, apparent from these lists of persons aiding in the royal coronation that both official and non-official or popular elements were represented in the function. The relation of jewels to the sovereign's

[1] Cf. *Atharvaveda* [iii. 1, 4, 2] :—

त्वां विशो वृणतां राज्याय = "the people elect you to rulership." In *Taittiriya Saṅhitā* [ii. 3, 1, 3] the Viś clearly means the people.

crown must also be implied to be the relation subsisting between the king on the one hand and the state functionaries and other popular representatives on the other. Each is necessary for the other.

The next interesting feature in the Rājasūya was the Abhiṣechanīyam, the consecration ceremony. It begins with the offerings to the Divine Quickeners, viz., Savitā Satyaprasava for righteous energy, Agni Gṛihapati for householders' prosperity, Soma Vanaspati for growth of trees (flora or agriculture), Bṛihaspati Vāk for power of speech, Indra for lordship, governing capacity, Rudra for cattle, Mitra for truth, and Varuna Dharmapati for protection of the law, since "that truly is the supreme state when one is lord of the law." Then follow the preparation of the consecration water, made up of no less than seventeen kinds (including the waters of dew, pond and sea); the sprinkling by a Brahman, a kinsman of the king-elect, a Kṣatriya nobleman (rājanya) and a Vaisya; the investing of the king with the consecration garments and with bow and arrows, three in number, as emblem of sovereignty, so as "to make all the quarters safe from arrows for him"; the announcements of the kingship to all classes of people, the Brahmans and Kṣatriyas, priesthood and nobility, and even animate and inanimate nature; the ascending of the quarters, East, South, West, North and upper region, so that "he is high above everything here and everything here is below him"; the anointing with the following significant formula[1]: "Quicken him, O Gods, to be unrivalled for great chiefdom, for great lordship, for the government of the people whose king he is—this man, O ye

[1] असपत्नं सुवद्ध्वमितीमं देवा अभ्रातृव्यं सुवद्ध्वमित्येवैतदाह महते क्षत्राय महते ज्यैष्ठ्यायेति नात्र तिरोहितमेवास्ति महते जानराज्यायेति महते जनानां राज्यायेत्येवैतदाहेन्द्रस्येन्द्रियायेति वीर्य्यायेत्येवैतदाह यदा हेन्द्रस्येन्द्रियायेति । [*Śatapatha*, v. 4, 2, 3.]

(Bharatāh in the *Taittiriya Sańhitā*), is your king . . . !"

XXIII

Besides the Vājapeya and the Rājasūya, we find two other forms of the inauguration of great kings described in the *Aitareya Brāhmaṇa.* They are called Punaraviṣekha· and Aindra-mahābhiṣekha. The object of these special consecrations is thus described:—The priest who wishes that his Kṣatriya king-elect should achieve all kinds of conquest, should know (by governing) all peoples, should attain to a position of leadership, precedence and superiority among kings, should secure sovereignty, a dominion of righteousness, absolute independence, highest distinction as a ruler, fulfilment of highest desires, the widest empire and highest authority, that he might be a universal overlord, with his powers reaching everywhere up to the limits of the sea, the sole master of his vast dominion—such a priest should inaugurate the Kshatriya with Indra's great inauguration ceremony, demanding from him a promise on oath that he will lose everything, even the accumulated fruits of his good deeds, all he has, even his life, if he attempts violation of right and truth.[1]

XXIV

The elaboration of the rituals connected with these imperial inaugurations,[2] which

[1] अहं सर्व्वेषां राज्ञां श्रैष्ठ्यमतिष्ठां परमतां गच्छेयं साम्राज्यं भोज्यं स्वाराज्यं वैराज्यं पारमेष्ठ्यं राज्यं माहाराज्यं आधिपत्यमहं समन्तपर्य्यायीस्यां सार्व्वभौमः सार्व्वायुष आन्तादा-परार्द्धात् पृथिव्यै समुद्रपर्य्यन्ताया एकराडिति ।

[2] Along with the ceremonies of the Vājapeya, Rājasūya, and Asvamedha should also be noticed the institution of Digvijaya, which was inseparable from the conception of a paramount sovereign in the popular Hindu mind. Sanskrit literature, epic, pauranic or classical, is full of references to this institution, and the more prominent examples of Digvijaya are those of Satrughna, Arjuna (see Jaimini Bhārata), Raghu (see Raghuvańsa), Pushpamitra (see Mālavikāgnimitra), Samudra Gupta, Harsavardhana, Gautamiputra Śatakarṇi, Pulakesi II., Lalitāditya of Kashmir (see Rāja-Tarangini), etc.

it is unnecessary to follow in greater detail for our present purpose, indicates without doubt the nature of the political environment in which it was developed, the height of the ideal which kingship in India had realised in practice. The geography of India has indeed partially influenced her history: her vast expanse had practically no limits in the eyes of the early settlers and colonisers; she was a world unto herself. An infinite stretch of territory produced a psychology, a philosophy that was easily dominated by a sense of the infinite and eternal.[1] The Hindu Ṛiṣi would recognise no limits to the development of his finite self. The Hindu king would also set no bounds to his political ambition. It was nothing short of universal sovereignty, which was reduced by the actualities of the objective environment into the sovereignty of the whole of India "up to the limits of

[1] For a similar sentiment, cf. Sister Niveditā's *The Web of Indian Life*, p. 143.

the ocean." The highest class in the hierarchy of Hindu kings was made up of those who were Āsamudrakṣitīsa ("आसमुद्रक्षितीश"). As the *Aitareya Brāhmaṇa* puts it: "Monarchy at its highest should have an empire extending right up to natural boundaries, it should be territorially all-embracing, up to the very ends uninterrupted, and should constitute and establish one state and administration in the land up to the seas" (VIII. 4, 1). Thus it was again his religion which put before the Hindu king the ideal of making the area of authority co-extensive with that of territory. The territorial synthesis leads the way to the political synthesis and is in turn emphasised by it.

XXV

Side by side with these ideals and conceptions of an all-India overlordship, the books also preserve for us traditional lists[1] of kings who are said to have succeeded in realising them in life—giving another proof that at least the conception of India, both as a political and geographical unit, was not foreign to Hindu consciousness. Such a list is to be found in the *Aitareya Brāhmaṇa* [VIII. 14, 4; 19, 2] and mentions the following great kings, each of whom achieved the singular distinction of "subjugating the whole country up to its farthest limits in every direction":—

(1) Janamejaya Pārikṣita with his priest Tura Kāvaṣeya.

(2) Śāryāta Mānava with his priest Chyavana Bhārgava.

(3) Śatānīka Sātrájita with his priest Somaśuṣmā Vājaratnāyana.

(4) Āmbāṣṭhya with his priests Parvata and Nārada.

[1] A comparative study of these lists in Sanskrit Literature will, however, tend to establish the historicity of these Indian great kings who preceded Chandragupta Maurya, the so-called *first* paramount sovereign of India. This should prove a very fruitful line of investigation.

(5) Yudhāṅśrauṣṭi Āugrasenya with the priests Parvata and Nārada.

(6) Visvakarmā Bhauvana with his priest Kaśyapa.

(7) Sudās Paijavana with his priest Vasiṣtha.

(8) Marutta Āvikṣita with his priest Sańvarta.

(9) Aṅga Vairochana with his priest Udamaya Ātreya. He is said to have made to his priests gifts of innumerable cows, 80,000 white horses, 10,000 elephants, etc.

(10) Bharata Dausmanti with his priest Dīrghatamā Māmateya. He is also said to have given away (i) innumerable elephants of black colour with white tusks and golden trappings in the country of Masñāra; (ii) innumerable cows to 1000 Brahmins of the country named Sāchīguna. He is also said to have kept 78 horses in a place on the Yamunā, and 55 in the place named Vṛitraghṇa on the Ganges for purposes of his horse-sacrifices,

and thus subdued the enemy's power. As the heavens are inaccessible to human hands, so was the height of Bharata's achievements to all classes of men—viz., the Brāhmanas, Kṣatriyas, Vaisyas, Sudras and Nisādas (Sāyana). It was this Bharata after whom Bhāratavarṣa was named as mentioned above.

(11) Durmukha Pāñchāla with his priest Bṛihaduktha.

(12) Atyarāti Jānantapi with his priest Vāsiṣṭha Sātyahavya. This king was afterwards deprived of his power for his breach of faith with his priest and was killed by his enemy Śaivya Śuṣmiṇa. The land of Uttarakuru is also referred to as unconquerable in the story.

Besides the list of great kings in the *Aitareya Brāhmaṇa* there is another list to be found in the *Śatapatha Brāhmaṇa* [XIII. 5, 4] of kings who performed the horse-sacrifice and were therefore recognised as paramount sovereigns. For the Asvamedha, as is well known, involved an assertion of power and a display of political authority such as only a monarch of undisputed supremacy could have ventured upon without courting humiliation. The ruling of the *Āpastamba Śrauta Sūtra* [XX. 1, 1] on the point may be quoted: "A king governing the whole land [Śarvabhauma सार्व्वभौम] may perform the Asvamedhá."[1] The

[1] "राजा सार्व्वभौमोऽश्वमेधेन यजेत ।"

The Asvamedha sacrifice was performed in the following manner:—"A horse of a particular colour was consecrated by the performance of certain ceremonies and was then turned loose to wander for a year. The king, or his representative, followed the horse with an army, and when the animal entered a foreign country the ruler of that country was bound either to fight or to submit. If the liberator of the horse succeeded in obtaining or enforcing the submission of all the countries over which it passed, he returned in triumph with all the vanquished Rājās in his train; but if he failed he was disgraced, and his pretensions ridiculed. After his successful return, a great festival was held at which the horse was sacrificed [Dowson, *Classical Dict.*]." In the Asvamedha of Yudhisthira the horse is guarded in its year's roaming by Arjuna, who first presses eastwards towards the sea, then turning southwards along the eastern shore as far as the extreme point of the peninsula, turns northwards on the homeward way, passing along the western coast.

list of these Asvamedhins is given as follows:—

1. Janamejaya Pārikṣita, with his Ṛiṣi Indrota Daivāpa Śaunaka.

2. Bhīmasena
3. Ugrasena
4. Śrutasena
} the Pārikṣitas.

5. Para Ātnāra, the Kausalya king.

6. Purukutsa, the Aikṣāka king.

7. Marutta Avikṣita, the Āyogava king.

8. Kraivya, the Pāñchāla king ("the Pāñchāla overlord of the Krivis").

The historical list of Asvamedhins includes the following names: (1) Pushyamitra [see Mālavikāgnimitra Act V.]; (2) Samudragupta [see Udayagiri Cave Inscription of Chandragupta II., L. 5; Bilsad Stone Inscription of Kumāragupta, L. 2, &c.]; (3) Kumāragupta I. and (4) Ādityasena [see V. A. Smith's *Early History of India*, p. 295]. On some of the gold coins which are attributed to Samudragupta, there occurs the legend asvamedha-parākramah (अश्वमेध-पराक्रम) "he who has displayed prowess by a horse-sacrifice." [See J. A. S. B. Volume LIII., Part I., p. 175 ff, and Pl. ii., No. 9; and Arch. Sur. West. Ind., Vol. II., p. 37f., and Pl. vii., No. 4.] Pulakesi I., the Chalukyan King, is also said to have performed a great Asvamedha or horse-sacrifice. [See Bhandarkar's *Early History of the Deccan*, p. 37.]

9. Dhvasan Dvaitavana, the king of the Matsyas.

10. Bharata Dauhṣanti ("who attained that wide sway which now belongs to the Bharatas"). He is said to have bound 78 steeds on the Yamunā and 55 near the Gangā and conquered the whole earth (cf. *Aitareya Br.* above).

11. Ṛiṣava Yājñātura.

12. Sātrāsāha, the Pāñchāla king.

13. Śatānīka Sātrājita.

The *Śankhāyana Śrauta Sutra* [XVI. 9] also preserves a similar list of Asvamedhins, which includes the following kings :—

1. Janamejaya
2. Ugrasena
3. Bhīmasena
4. Śrutasena

} Pārikṣitas.

5. Ṛiṣava Yājnātura.
6. Vaideha Alhāra.
7. Marutta Āvikṣita.

XXVI

These lists of great kings preserved in Vedic literature are also supplemented by other lists in the Purāṇas and other works. The Kūrma Purāṇa [XX. 31] mentions King Vasumanā; the Padma Purāṇa mentions King Dilīpa and his predecessors Manu, Sagara, Marutta and Yayāti [IV. 110–118]; while the Agni Purāṇa [ch. 219, 50–51] mentions Pṛithu, Dilīpa, Bharata, Valī, Malla, Kakustha, Yuvanāsva, Jayadratha, Māndhātā, Muchukunda, Pururavāh. The Brahma Purāṇa mentions Pururavāh, who is called Pṛithivīpati[1] (पृथिवीपति), Bhīma, called Rājarāt,[2] Yayāti,[3] who subdued the earth up to the seas, Kārtavīrya-Arjuna,[4] who is called Samrātchakravartī. The Brahmāṇḍa Purāṇa mentions Pṛithu.[5] The Mārkaṇḍeya mentions Pururavāh[6]

[1] X. 9. [2] X. 13. [3] XII. 18.
[4] XIII. 174. [5] LXIX. 1, 2, 3. [6] CXI. 13.

as Chakravarttī and Marutta.[1] The Śiva Purāṇa mentions Chitraratha,[2] Pṛithu[3] as Chakravarttī, and Hariśchandra[4] as Samrāt. The Liṅga Purāṇa mentions Yayāti,[5] Kārtavīrya-Arjuna,[6] Śaśavinda,[7] and Uśanā.[8] The Skanda-Purāṇa mentions Kārtavīrya[9] as Samrāt Chakravarttī. The Bhāgavata Purāṇa mentions Māndhātā[10] and Sagara[11] as Chakravarttī and Muchukunda[12] as Akhandabhūmipa. The Devīpurāṇa uses the word Ekarāt[13] in respect of a Daitya named Ghora. The Viṣṇu-purāṇa mentions Sagara,[14] Chandra,[15] Bharata,[16] Mahāpadma Nanda,[17] and Chandragupta.[18] The Vāyu mentions Sagara,[19] Kārtavīrya-Arjuna[20] and Uśanā.[21] The Matsya mentions Pururavāh[22] and Puru,[23] the son of Yayāti.

[1] CXXXII. 3, 4. [2] XXIV. 34, 35. [3] *Ibid.* 65, 66.
[4] LXI. 21. [5] LXVI. [6] LXVIII.
[7] LXVIII. [8] *Ibid.* [9] *Pravāsa-khaṇḍa*, XX. 11, 12.
[10] IX. vi. 34. [11] *Ibid.* 4. [12] X. li. 14.
[13] II. 39. [14] III. iv. 17. [15] VI. iv. 6.
[16] XIX. iv. 2. [17] XXIV. iv. 5. [18] XXIV. iv. 7.
[19] LXXXVIII. 144. [20] XCIV. 9.
[21] XCV. 23. [22] XXIV. 11. [23] XXXIV. 25.

The Mahābhārata in many places refers to the great Indian kings of old. A complete enumeration of them is contained in the Śantiparva [ch. XXIX.], where the following kings are named :—

1. Marutta, son of Avikṣita.

2. Suhotra, son of Atithi.

3. Bṛihadrâtha, the King of the Angas.

4. Śivi, the son of Uśinara, "who swayed the whole earth as one sways the leathern shield, and the wheels of whose victorious chariot rolled unopposed over the whole earth, who brought the whole earth under one authority,"[1] etc.

5. Bharata, the son of Dusmanta and Sakuntalā, who, as stated above

[1] य इमां पृथिवीं सर्व्वां चर्म्मवत् समवेष्टयत् ।
महता रथघोषेण पृथिवीमनुनादयन् ।
एकच्छत्रां मही चक्रे जैत्रेणैकरथेन यः ॥
[39–41]

in the Aitareya Brāhmaṇa, sacrificed three hundred horses on the banks of the Yamunā, twenty on the Sarasvatī, and fourteen on the Gaṅgā.[1]

6. Rāma, son of Daśaratha.

7. Bhagīratha of Ikṣāku dynasty.

8. Dilīpa.

9. Māndhātā, son of Yuvanāśva, who subdued the whole earth and vanquished the following kings, viz., Angāra, Marutta, Asita, Gaya and Brihadratha, the King of the Aṅgas,[2] and on whose wide empire "the sun never sets."

10. Yayāti, son of Nahūṣa, who con-

[1] यो बद्धा त्रिशतं चाश्वान् देवेभ्यो यमुनामनु
सरस्वतीं विंशतिश्च गङ्गामनु चतुर्द्दश ॥
[46]

[2] तस्मिमं पृथिवी सर्व्वा एकाह्नासमपद्यत ।
यस्याङ्गारस्तु नृपतिं मरुत्तमसितं गयम् ।
अङ्गं बृहद्रथञ्चैव मान्धाता समरेऽजयत् ॥
* * *
यत्र सूर्य्य उदेतिस्म यत्र च प्रतितिष्ठति ।
सर्व्वं तद्यौवनाश्वस्य मान्धातुः क्षेत्रमुच्यते ॥
[87, 88, 90]

quered the whole earth up to the seas and performed a hundred Vājapeyas.[1]

11. Ambarīṣa, the son of Nābhāga, the king of innumerable kings.[2]

12. Śaśavindu, the son of Chitraratha.

13. Gaya, the son of Amurtharayaś.

14. Rantideva, son of Saukriti.

15. Sagara, of Ikṣāku dynasty, whose sway extended over the whole earth.[3]

16. Pṛithu, the son of Vena.

The *Arthaśāstra* of Kauṭilya also gives expression to the conception of an all-India overlord and a list of kings who

[1] य इमां पृथिवीं कृत्स्नां विजित्य सह सागराम् ।

* * *

व्यभजत् पृथिवीं कृत्स्नां ययातिर्नहुषात्मजः ॥

[94, 97]

[2] यः सहस्रं सहस्राणां राज्ञामयुतयाजिनाम् ।

* * *

शतं राजसहस्राणि शतं राजशतानि च

सर्व्वेऽश्वमेधैरीजानास्तेऽन्वयुर्दक्षिणायनम् ॥

[101, 103]

[3] एकच्छत्रा मही यस्य प्रतापादभवत् पुरा ।

[132]

realised that ideal. The paramount sovereign is called *chāturantorājā* (चातुरन्तो राजा) [Mysore edition, p. 11], *i.e.*, whose dominion extends up to the farthest limits in the four quarters of the country; he is also represented as governing the whole country with none to dispute his right ("अनन्यां पृथिवीं भुंक्ते") [*ibid.*]. His dominion (*chakravarti kṣetram* चक्रवर्त्तिक्षेत्रम्) is specially defined as the country between the Himalayas and the ocean, which is an evident reference to Chandragupta's sovereignty [हिमवत्समुद्रान्तरं चक्रवर्त्तिक्षेत्रं (Mysore ed., p. 33)]. There is a list of kings which includes the following names: (1) Dāṇdyakya-Bhoja, (2) Vaideha-karāla, (3) Janamejaya, (4) Tālajangha, (5) Aila, (6) Ajavindu-Sauvira, (7) Rāvaṇa, (8) Duryodhana, (9) Ḍambodbhava, (10) Haihaya-Arjuna, (11) Vātāpi. These kings all failed to be great because of their want of self-control and subjection of the senses. Among the successful great kings are named Ambarīṣa and Nābhāga [see pp. 11, 12, Mysore ed.].

XXVII

Following this long line of great Indian kings we come across the illustrious name of Yudhiṣṭhira, who proclaimed his over-lordship and paramount-power before the Imperial Durbar at Indraprastha, to which were invited kings from the remotest parts of India and beyond to render him homage and realise the unity of that vast empire into which were federated their smaller kingdoms. For the Mahābhārata preserves for us a picture of India that was divided politically into innumerable small states, kingdoms and republics, whose mutual jealousies and animosities afterwards culminated in the Great War of the Mahābhārata. It was left to the superior power of Yudhiṣṭhira to arrest these disruptive tendencies for a time by the evolution of a peaceful confederation in which every state was kept in its proper sphere and orbit to promote the larger life of the whole. That this task of political reconstruction was not an easy one, that the ancient Śāstric ideal of kingship of bringing the whole country "up to the sea" under the yoke of a common authority was difficult to achieve was thus recognised by Yudhiṣṭhira [Sabhā parva, XV. 2]: "There are kings everywhere living independently, doing what they like, but they have not attained to the rank of emperor, for that appellation is difficult to obtain."[1] The situation was indeed full of difficulties. There were powerful kings on every side aiming at overlordship. To the north there was Hastināpura, the capital of the Kurus. To the east Mathurā was held by a powerful sovereign. To the south the King of Mālava was a standing menace,

[1] "गृहे गृहे हि राजानः स्वस्य स्वस्य प्रियंकराः ।
न च साम्राज्यमाप्तास्ते सम्राट्शब्दो हि कृच्छ्रभाक् ॥"

and to the west there was the principality of Virāṭa equally ambitious. There were other mighty kings in different parts of India, but the most powerful of them was Jarāsandha, King of Magadha, who aspired to suzerainty. His subjugation was the first achievement of the Pāṇḍus in their career of an all-India conquest, and four grand military expeditions were then organised, one to proceed to each quarter of India. Arjuna assumed the command of the northern advance, and to his might fell victims the Kulindas, the Kālakutas, the Avarthas, the Śvākala-dvipis; Bhagadatta of Prāgjyotiṣa; the Himalayan chiefs such as those of Uluka, Modapura, Vainadeva, Sudāman, Susankula, Devaprastha, etc.; also the Kirātas and the Chīnas. Arjuna then turned towards the west through Kāshmir to Balkh and, on his way back, through Kamboja, Darada, etc. Across the Himalayas were encountered the kings of Kimpilla-varṣa and Hālaka near Mānasa lake and, lastly,

Uttarakuru. The second expedition was led by Bhima towards the east, subduing Drupada, Daśārna, the Pulindas, Chedi, Kosala, Ayodhyā, Uttara Kosala, Urulla and the Terai ; then Kasi, the Matṣyas, the Maladas, Madadhāras, the Vatsabhumiyas, the Bhangas, the Santakas and Varmakas, and several Kirāta and other races. Mithilā courted alliance and Magadha paid tribute. Then the country of Karṇa (Bhagalpur) was subdued and subsequently the petty chiefs of Vaṅga. The southern advance was under Sahadeva, who similarly marched victorious through many petty kingdoms and, crossing the Narmadā, passed through Kiṣkindhā, Mahiṣmati to Southern India, securing the allegiance of Dravida, Sarabhipattanam, Tāmra island, Timingila (the country of the whale), Kaliṅga, Andhra, Udra, Kerala, Tālavana, Ceylon and other places. On his way home, he passed along the western coast through Surat to Guzrat, and finally returned home, laden with wealth and presents. Nakula, leading the western expedition, passed through Rohitaka and thence Southern Rajputana to Mahettha, Sivi, Trigarta, Ambastha, Mālava, Pañchkaiphatas, Mādhyamaka, Vàtadhāna; thence he turned towards Puṣkara and, through the Abhira country, marched on to the Punjab and encountered in the north-west the Pallavas, Barbaras, Kirātas, Yavanas and the Śakas, from all of whom he obtained valuable presents and acknowledgment of allegiance.

Thus the whole of India for the time resounded with the din of the conquering marches of the Pāṇḍavas asserting the authority of a superior power; the whole country was united in submission to a sovereign claiming its homage and alliance. India once again was imagined and used as a political unit; the different parts were integrated into a federal whole: the separated lives of the provinces were united in a common life.

XXVIII

The story of Yudhiṣṭhira known to every Hindu has accordingly immensely popularised the old Vedic conception of an all-India sovereignty of which Yudhiṣṭhira was such a prominent embodiment. The idea became one of the current political notions of the ancient Hindus, not a subject of thought but an integral part of thought. It lost none of its strength in later times. It had sufficient vitality to stamp its impress on the earliest Buddhist thought. We are generally familiar with the influences of Hinduism on Buddhism; we know how Buddhism is rooted deep in the religious speculation of the Hindus. But we do not know that some of the fundamental religious conceptions of the Buddhists were inspired by Hindu *political* thought as distinguished from Hindu religious thought.

For the early Buddhist ideas of the Buddha were dominated by the then prevailing Hindu ideal of the chakravarti Rājā to which the Buddha was always thought and described to conform. The Hindu ideal was understood by the Buddhists and explained in the early Suttas to be that of "a King of Kings, a righteous man who ruled in righteousness, lord of the four quarters of the earth, invincible, the protector of his people, possessor of the seven royal treasures."[1]

The first of these treasures was the treasure of the wheel which is represented to roll onwards, like the sun in old Vedic poetry, to the very extremities of the world conquering and to conquer.[2] The

[1] *Mahā-Sudassana Sutta* in S. B. E., Vol. xi., p. 248.

[2] Cf. *Rig-veda* [vii. 32, 20]: "The much-landed Indra I incline by means of the song as a cartwright bends the rim of a wheel made of good wood"; and also [i. 32, 35] "the lightning in his hand rules over all men as the rim of a wheel embraces the spokes." In the *Sutta* the wheel is represented to have rolled towards the East, South, West and North followed by the Emperor to whom "all rival kings became subject."

second treasure of the King of Kings is the white elephant which can carry its master across the broad earth to its very ocean boundary like the Airāvata of Indra, "the personification of the great white, fertilising rain-cloud so rapid in its passage before the winds of the monsoon over the vault of heaven." The third treasure was the treasure of the horse, probably also derived from the Vedic "charger-King whose name was thunder-cloud." The fourth was the treasure of the gem called the *Veluriya* (from which the word *beryl* is probably derived), "the splendour of which spread round about a league every side," like the jewel of lightning with which Indra in the Vedas slays the demon of darkness. Fifthly, the King of Kings is the possessor of a pearl among women; and the two last treasures are a *treasurer* and an *adviser*, faithful servants, like the pearl among women, of the king of kings.

Such a king of kings the early Buddhists saw in Buddha who became the ruler of a supernatural world,[1] an empire of truth; whose wheel was the wheel of the Dharma which the King of Righteousness himself had set rolling onwards, that wheel which will roll over all the world, unchecked in its course; whose Prime Minister was his chief disciple Śariputta; and whose teaching, like rain cloud, rained down the ambrosia of bliss, fertilising right desires, extinguishing the fires of lust, hatred and ignorance.

Thus the old Hindu conception of a paramount overlordship having reference to an actual empire was seized by early Buddhist thought to describe its achievement which resulted in the foundation of an ideal empire, the empire of righteousness in the hearts of men. The Hindu Chakravarttī was he who made

[1] Cf. *Selasutta in Suttanipāta* [III. 7, 7]: "A King am I, Sela, the King Supreme Of Righteousness. The royal chariot wheel In righteousness do I set rolling on—that wheel that no one can turn back again."

the wheels of his chariot roll unopposed over all the world; the wheel was the symbol of his power. But Buddha was a different kind of Chakravarttī: he who set rolling the royal chariot-wheel of a universal empire of truth and righteousness. His wheel was the symbol not of power but of Dharma. His work is accordingly described as *Dhamma chakkappavattana*, which is the name given to the famous Sutta in which is embodied the very essence of Buddha's teachings.[1]

XXIX

It is thus abundantly clear that in the days of ancient Buddhism the whole of India was comprehended as a single territory to be brought within the scope of one all-embracing authority though the conception was expanded and idealised by Buddhist religious fervour. And

[1] See Rhys Davids, *Hibbert Lecture*, pp. 129 and 4, *Buddhism*, pp. 45, 46, 220, and *S. B. E.*, Vol. XI.

Chandra Gupta was thus not the first to conceive and realise the ideal of paramount sovereignty, but only came into the possession of a rich inheritance which his genius utilised and improved to the fullest extent. His success naturally contributed a good deal to the strength and popularity of the ideal he represented and realised. The problem "How can a king become a king of kings?" soon became a favourite familiar topic of discussion in the ancient schools of political thought. It gave rise to much scientific, systematic speculation, which was embodied in the theory of the Maṇḍala or Circle of Kings as outlined in the works on Nīti-Śāstra. We find expositions of this theory both in the Arthaśāstra of Kauṭilya and the Nīti-Sāra of Kāmandaka in which there are also references to earlier authorities. The theory postulates the natural inevitable desire of small kings to become great and finds in that instinct the regulative principle or law which rules the political world in almost the same sense as gravitation rules the physical; which determines the evolution of states and the growth of empires and establishes a stable equilibrium and a balance of power.

The whole country is conceived of as a political circle (मण्डल) at the centre of which is the head (मण्डलाधिप), who is technically called Vijigīṣu (विजिगीषु), the would-be conqueror, who is to emerge as the paramount power dominating the system, who "shines in his sphere like the full moon."[1] The normal political circle is that formed by twelve kings,[2] including the central victorious king or sovereign, round whom are ranged, both in the front and rear, nine subordinate kings in varying degrees of friendliness and hostility, and two neutral kings (called

[1] *Kāmandaki*, VIII. 2, 3.

रथी विराजते राजा विशुद्धे मण्डले चरन्
रोचते सर्व्वभूतेभ्यः शशीवाखण्डमण्डलः ।

[2] सर्व्वलोकप्रतीतं तु स्फुटं द्वादशराजकम्—[*Ibid.* 41.]

मध्यम and उदासीन). This confederation of twelve kingdoms connected with one another by all possible kinds of political relationship is regarded as an approximation to the actual state of things, a map of the actual political situation, showing also its possible developments due to all conceivable changes of attitude of the component units. Thus the variations of the normal political system have been noticed by the ancient authors of polity. Kauṭilya[1] mentions a confederation or circle of three kings who may constitute a "sphere of influence"; Maya[2] of four kings (चतुष्कमण्डल); Pulomā[3] of six kings; Bṛihaspati[4] of eighteen kings; and Viśālākṣa[5] of fifty-four kings, and so forth. Thus the central monarch will find his sphere of action embracing both friendly and hostile kingdoms,[6] but if he is self-

[1] "विजिगीषुर्मित्रं मित्रमित्रं वाऽस्य प्रकृतयः तिस्रः।"
[*Arthaśāstra*, VI. ii. 17.]

[2] *Kāmandaki*, VIII. 20.

[3] *Ibid.* 71. [4] *Ibid.* 26. [5] *Ibid.* 28.

[6] *Ibid.* 21: "आकीर्णं मण्डलं सर्व्वं मित्रैररिभिरेव च।"

possessed, strong in all the elements of sovereignty, he is bound to achieve pre-eminence and attain to suzerainty ("एकैश्वर्य")[1] by his superior policy and statecraft, which by a proper manipulation of the various political forces can easily render his own position invincible, supreme and paramount.[2]

[1] *Arthaśāstra*, V., vi., 14, 15. The "elements of sovereignty" are "स्वाम्यमात्यजनपददुर्गकोशदण्डमित्राणि," *i.e.*, the king, the minister, the country (which by the way should have capital cities both in the centre and the extremities of the kingdom—"मध्ये चान्ते च स्थानवान"), the fort, the treasury, the army, and the ally.

[2] Cf. *Kāmandaki*, VIII. 83:

इति स्म राजा नयवर्त्मना व्रजन्
समुद्यमी मण्डलशुद्धिमाचरन् ।
विराजते साधु विशुद्धमण्डलः
शरच्छशीव प्रतिनन्दयन् प्रजाः ॥

Also *Arthaśāstra*, VI. i. 17:

"आत्मवांस्त्वल्पदेशोऽपि युक्तः प्रकृति-सम्पदा ।
नयज्ञः पृथिवीं कृत्स्नां जयत्येव न हीयते ॥"

Again [VI. ii. 17]:

नेमिमेकान्तरान् राज्ञः कृत्वा चानन्तरानरान्
नाभिमात्मानमायच्छेत् नेता प्रकृतिमण्डले ॥

("The leader of the confederation or circle of states

XXX

But the ideal of a paramount sovereign dominating the whole of India, besides expressing itself in literature, utters itself in no uncertain tones through some of the early Indian epigraphic records. Thus the term Mahārāja (महाराज), *lit.*, a great king, was used as one of the titles of paramount sovereignty by Kaniska, Huviska, and Vāsudeva, who, there is every reason to believe, were paramount sovereigns, in their inscriptions of the years 9, 39, and 83.[1] It is also used, in conjunction with the higher title of Rājātirāja, "superior king of kings," by the same three kings in their inscriptions

---

will make himself the nave of a wheel, of which the rim or circumference will be formed by the combination of friendly chiefs (lit., those kings who are separated from the central king by another king) and the spokes by the inimically inclined chiefs and will thus control the whole system.")

[1] *Arch. Sur. Ind.*, Vol. III., p. 31, Pl. XIII., No. 4; p. 32, Pl. XIV., No. 9; and p. 34, Pl. XV., No. 16.

of the years 11, 47, and 87.[1] In still earlier days the same title Mahārāja, in conjunction sometimes with the title Rājātirāja, and sometimes with Rājarāja (राजराज), "king of kings" (the two together being equivalent to the Greek *basileus basileon*), was used on the bilingual coins of Hemokadphises[2] (in conjunction with Rājātirāja) and of Azes[3] (in conjunction with Rājarāja). It was also used by itself to represent the Greek *basileus* on the coins of Hermaeus. The title Rājādhirāja occurs by itself on some of the coins of Maues[4] and in conjunction with the title Mahārājā on some of the coins of Azes,[5] while Rājātirāja occurs in the same sense but coupled with Mahārāja in the Mathura inscription of Huviska[6]

[1] *Arch. Sur. Ind.*, Vol. III., p. 33, Pl. XIV., No. 12 and p. 35, Pl. XV., No. 18.

[2] Gardner and Poole's *Catalogue* of Coins of the Greek and Scythic Kings of Bactria and India, p. 124 ff.

[3] *Ibid.*, p. 73 ff.

[4] *Ibid.*, p. 68 ff., Nos. 4, 5, 9, 11, and 17.

[5] *Ibid.*, p. 85 ff., Nos. 138, 140, and 157.

[6] *Arch: Sur. Ind.*, Vol. III., p. 33, No. 12, and Pl. XIV.

of the year 47 and of Vāsudeva[1] of the year 87.

In the inscriptions of the Guptas the following titles are used to indicate supreme paramount sovereignty, viz., Mahārājādhirāja (महाराजाधिराज), Parameśvara (परमेश्वर), Paramabhattāraka (परमभट्टारक), Rājādhirāja (राजाधिराज) and Chakravartin (चक्रवर्त्तिन). Thus the Allahabad posthumous stone pillar inscription of Samudragupta refers to him as "the Mahārājādhirāja, the glorious Samudragupta," and to his "conquest of the whole world." It also refers to him as "the son of the Mahārājādhirāja, the glorious Chandragupta I." and "the Mahādevi Kumāradevi,"[2] and

[1] *Arch. Sur. Ind.*, Vol. III., p. 35, No. 18, and Pl. XV.

[2] "... महाराजाधिराजश्री-चन्द्रगुप्त-पुत्रस्य-महादेव्यां-कुमार-देव्यां-उत्पन्नस्य-महाराजाधिराज-श्री-समुद्रगुप्तस्य-सर्व्वपृथिवी-विजय-जनितोदय-व्याप्त-निखिलावनी-तलम् ..."

Mahadevi was a technical title of the wives of paramount sovereigns along with Paramabhattārikā and Rājñī [cf. Mandar Hill Inscriptions of Ādityasena, Nos. 44 and 45 and Deo. Baranark inscription of Jīvitagupta II., No. 46 in *Corpus. Ins. Ind.*, Vol. III.].

also to Chandragupta II. as Paramabhattāraka.[1] The *Eran stone inscription* of Samudragupta compares him with the great ancient monarchs Prithu and Rāghava,[2] and refers to his subjugation of "the whole tribe of kings upon the earth."[3]

The Udayagiri cave inscription of Chandragupta II. refers to him as Paramabhattāraka and Mahārājādhirāja. The Mathurā stone inscription of Chandragupta II. refers to both Samudragupta and Chandragupta I. as Mahārājādhirāja, and to himself as the exterminator of all kings, who had no antagonist (of equal power) in the world and whose fame extended up to the shores of the four oceans,[4] and who was the restorer of the

[1] L. 33 of the inscription.

[2] L. 8—"नृपतयः पृथु-राघवाद्याः . . ."

[3] L. 11—"पार्थिव-गणस्सकलः पृथिव्यां . . ."

[4] L. 1, 2,—

"सर्व्वराजोच्छेत्तुः पृथिव्यामप्रतिरथस्य चतुरुदधिसलिला-स्वादित-यशसो . . ." L. 5—"अश्वमेधाहर्त्तुः . . ."

asvamedha-sacrifice that had been long in abeyance. The Sanchi stone inscription of Chandragupta II. also refers to him as Mahārājādhirāja, who has acquired banners of victory and fame in many battles.[1] Another Udayagiri cave inscription of Chandragupta II. refers to the purchase-money of his prowess which bought the earth and made slaves of all kings,[2] and uses the epithet Rājādhirāja. The Gaḍhwa stone inscription of Chandragupta II. refers to him as Mahārājādhirāja.[3]

Kumaragupta is referred to as Mahārājadhirāja in the two Gadhwa stone inscriptions[4]; also in the Bilsad stone pillar inscription,[5] which applies the epithet to his ancestors Chandragupta II.,[6] Samudragupta,[7] and Chandragupta I.,

[1] L. 4—
"... अनेक-समरावाप्त-विजय-यशस्-पताकाः ..."

[2] L. 2—
"विक्रम-व्यावक्रय-क्रीड़ादास्य-न्यक्भूत-पार्थिवा ..."

[3] L. 1 and L. 10.

[4] L. 1 in both the inscriptions.

[5] L. 5. [6] L. 6. [7] L. 4.

and makes a special reference to Samudragupta as the restorer of Asvamedha sacrifice.[1] The Mankuwur stone image inscription of Kumāragupta, however, refers to him only as a Mahārāja, which was then a subordinate feudatory title, either by a mistake or because of the reduction of Kumāragupta to feudal rank by the Pusyamitras and the Hunas. The Mandasor stone inscription also refers to Kumāragupta as reigning over the whole earth.[2]

Skandagupta is called Mahārājādhirāja in the Bihar stone inscription,[3] which repeats the usual ancestral references and exploits. The Bhitari stone pillar inscription refers to him as the most eminent hero in the lineage of the Guptas,[4] who by his conquests "subju-

[1] L. 2—"... अश्वमेधाहर्त्तुः..."

[2] "पृथिवीं प्रशासति"—L. 13.

[3] L. 22.

[4] L. 7—"... गुप्तवंशैकवीरः..."

gated the earth,"[1] and repeats the ancestral exploits. The Junagadh rock inscription calls him Rājarājādhirāj,[2] who "made subject to himself the whole earth bounded by the waters of the four oceans,"[3] who "destroyed the height of the pride of his enemies and appointed protectors in all the countries;[4] who is the banner of his lineage, the lord of the whole earth; whose pious deeds are even more wonderful than his supreme sovereignty over kings,"[5] etc. The Kahaum stone pillar inscription refers to him as the lord of a hundred kings, "whose hall of audience is shaken by the wind caused by the falling down (in the act of performing

[1] L. 14—"... यो बाहुभ्यामवनीं विजित्य ..."

[2] L. 2.

[3] "... चतुरुदधिजलान्तां-स्फीत-पर्य्यन्तदेशं अवनीमवनतारिर्यः ..."

[4] L. 6—"... एवं स जित्वा पृथिवीं समग्रां-भग्नाग्रदर्पान्-द्विषतस्च-कृत्वा-सर्व्वेषु देशेषु विधाय गोप्तृन ..."

[5] L. 24—"दृप्तारिदर्पप्रणुदः पृथुश्रियः - स्ववंशकेतोः - सकलावनी-पतेः—राजाधिराज्याद्भुत-पुण्यकर्म्मणः ..."

obeisance) of the heads of those hundred kings."[1] The *Indor copper-plate inscription* of Skandagupta applies to him the titles Paramabhattāraka and Mahārājādhirāja, and speaks of his "augmenting victorious reign."[2]

The Meherauli posthumous iron pillar inscription of Chandra refers to him as having attained sole supreme sovereignty in the world and "the breezes of his prowess by which the southern ocean is even still perfumed," who crossed the seven mouths of the Indus and conquered the Vāhlikas.[3]

The Mandasor stone pillar inscription of Yasordharman describes him as a paramount sovereign holding sway over a large

[1] L. 1—"यस्योपस्थानभूमिर्नृपतिशतशिरः पातवाताबधूत..." L. 3—क्षितिपशतपतेः..."

[2] L. 3—"... परमभट्टारक-महाराजाधिराज-श्रीस्कन्दगुप्तस्याभि-वर्द्धमाण-विजयराज्य..."

[3] L. 2—"तीर्त्वा सप्तमुखानि येन समरे सिन्धोर्जिता वाह्लिकायस्याद्याप्यधिवास्यते जलनिधिर्वीर्य्यानिलैर्दक्षिणः।" L. 5—"... ऐकाधिराज्यं क्षितौ ... ।"

part of India from the river Lauhitya or the Brahmaputra to the western ocean and from the Himalayas to the mountain Mahendra. He is described as falling but little short of Manu and Bharata, Alarka and Māndhātṛi, the great kings of old, in whom the title of "universal sovereign" shines most.[1]

Another Maṇdasor stone inscription of Viṣṇuvardhana applies to him the titles of Rājādhirāja and Paramesvara, and refers to his subjection of many mighty kings of the east and north.[2]

The long Alina copper-plate inscription of Siladitya VII. applies the epithets Paramabhattāraka, Mahārājādhirāja, Parameśvara and Chakravartin to Dharasena IV. and the first three epithets to

[1] L. 3—"... स श्रेयो-धाम्नि-सम्राड़िति मनु-भरतालर्कमान्धातृकल्पे कल्याणे हेम्नि भास्वन्-मणिरिव सुतरां भ्राजते यत्र शब्दः।"

[2] L. 6—"... प्राचो नृपान् सुबृहतश्च बहूनुदीचाः साम्ना युधा च वशगान् प्रविधाय येन नामापरं जगति कान्तमदो दुरापं राजाधिराजपरमेश्वर इत्युदूढ़म्।"

Śilādityadeva III., Śilādityadeva IV., Śilādityadeva V., Śilādityadeva VI., and Śilādityadeva VII.

The Mandar Hill rock inscription of Adityasena applies to him the paramount titles Paramabhattāraka and Mahārājādhirāja.

The Deo-Baranark inscription of Jivita-Gupta II. uses the paramount titles Paramabhattāraka, Mahārājādhirāja and Paramesvara in respect of Devaguptadeva, Visnuguptadeva and Jivitaguptadeva II.

The Sonpat copper seal inscription of Harsavardhana applies the paramount titles Paramabhattāraka and Mahārājādhirāja to Prabhākaravardhana, Rajyavardhana II., and Harsavardhana.

The copper-plate inscription of Samudragupta discovered at Gayā repeats the paramount title Mahārājādhirāja and the achievements of Samudragupta and his ancestors.

Some of the historical inscriptions in the cave-temples of Western India contain references to titles of paramount sovereignty used by some successful kings. In the longest of the four inscriptions at Nasik of Gotamiputra[1] Śātakarni and Pulumāyi, Gotamiputra is spoken of as "king of kings," whose exploits rivalled those of Rāma, Kesava, Arjūna, Bhimasena: whose prowess was equal to that of Nābhāga, Naḥūsa, Janamejaya, Sagara, Yayāti, Rāma and Ambarīṣa. The inscriptions of Pulakeśi II. (A.D. 611–634) show his assumption of the imperial title Paramesvara, lord paramount. Both Dantidurga, the Rāshtrakuta monarch who overthrew the Chalukyas, and his son Kriṣṇarāja is spoken of in their copper-plate grants as having become paramount sovereigns. Their successor, Govinda III., is also made out by his Baroda copper-plate grant to have been a paramount king making and unmaking subordinate kings.

Some of the Bengal Pāla kings also

[1] *Arch. Sur. W. Ind.*, No. 26.

used paramount titles of sovereignty as shown by their inscriptions. Thus a Nālanda inscription refers to Gopāla as Paramabhattāraka Mahārājādhiraja Parameśvara. Another of Buddha Gayā speaks of "Paramabhattāraka—Śrimān Mahipāla Deva." In a copper-plate inscription at Monghyr Gopāla is called "king of the world" and "likened unto Prithu, Sagara and others."[1]

XXXI

Thus early Hindu history unmistakably shows that the political consciousness of the people had from very early times grasped the whole of India as a unit, and assimilated the entire area as the theatre of its activities. But the tide of life that was pulsating through India from end to

[1] *Arch. Sur. Ind.*, Vol. III., pp. 114, 120, 122. There are many other Pāla and other inscriptions in which there is a reference to paramount sovereignty or mention of paramount titles. It is needless for our purposes to refer to them all.

end, unifying and integrating its parts and varieties into one mighty organism, came inevitably in course of time to overflow its original geographical limits and spread itself over other lands. Indeed, there can hardly be a more convincing proof of the reality and strength of Indian unity than the story of Indian colonising activity and the gradual development of a Greater India across the seas. This is not the proper place[1] and occasion for the unfolding of that interesting history in all its details which is still one of the unillumined chapters of Indian history, and I content myself with stating here only the general conclusions and facts that stand out clear and definite. India for centuries sent out streams of colonists and emigrants to countries in the Far East, including Pegu, Siam, and Cambodia on the mainland, and to Java, Sumatra, Bali and Borneo

[1] The writer has under preparation a work on *Greater India.* See chapters in his *History of Indian Shipping, etc.* (Longmans, London), apposite to the subject.

among the islands of the Malay Archipelago, and "the reality of the debt due to India by those distant lands is attested abundantly by material remains, by the existence to this day of both the Buddhist and Brahmanical religions in the island of Bali to the east of Java, by Chinese history and by numerous traditions preserved in India, Pegu, Siam and the Archipelago."[1] This colonising activity resulted in the practical Indianisation of the countries touched by it—the transplantation, and in some cases reproduction, of Indian art,[2] institutions and even

[1] V. A. Smith's *A History of Fine Art, etc.*, p. 259.

[2] In Java the forms of art are thoroughly Indian in subject and style (see V. A. Smith's *A History of Fine Art, etc.*, pp. 259 and ff.). Of the monument of Borobudur, presenting no less than 2,000 bas-reliefs, the best reliefs, numbering more than 200, are arranged in two series, of which the upper presents in easily recognisable stone pictures the life of Buddha as told in the ancient Sanskrit work *Lalita Vistara*, while the lower has been proved to be an illustration of scenes from the *Divyā-vadāna* and other Buddhist romances, including some of the *Jātakas*. As regards other monuments, the following remarks of Mr. Sewell may be quoted: "Brambanam and Chandisewa are to all external

geographical names.[1] It is well known that some of the triumphs and masterpieces of India Art exist outside India in those countries which came within her

[1] According to Fergusson, the name Cambodia was given to a portion of Cochin-China by immigrants from Kamboja, *i.e.*, from the Kabul valley. Among other geographical names introduced into Java and Cambodia may be mentioned Gandhara, Taxila, Hastinagara or Hastinapura, Rumadesa (apparently the South Punjab), Ayodhya (the capital of Siam), and Intha-patha-puri (Indraprastha), the later capital of Cambodia.

---

appearances purely Brahmanical, though we learn on examination that Brahma, Visnu and Siva were there held to be Bodhisattvas and not gods. And this is the case everywhere in Eastern Java, the temples being mostly Hindu in type (though always with a difference), and having statues adapted generally from Brahmanical originals."

The ruins at Angkor-Wat in Cambodia are also distinctively of ancient Indian origin.

Siamese annals date from A.D. 685, the colonisation from India of Burma, Pegu, Siam and Cambodia. In Cambodia, however, the earliest recorded Indian ruler was Srutavarman in the middle of the fifth century, followed by Bhavavarman, who founded many temples in honour of Indian deities, especially Siva, at which daily readings of the epics and *Puranas* were held. Indian influence was at its height in Cambodia in the sixth century [*Kern* quoted by V. A. Smith, *A History of Fine Art, etc.*, p. 261]. Traditions of the migrations from India to Indo-China date them from a much earlier influence, while the ideas and institutions travelled with the spread of Buddhism,

---

period. The earliest is the mythic account of the conversion of Indo-China to Buddhism before the time of Asoka. Probably the eastward colonisation was originally begun by the Dravidians in the pre-Christian era and continued in subsequent periods. Next, a migration in the first century A.D. of Yavanas or Śakas from Tamluk or Ratnāvati on the Hugli is in agreement with the large number of Indian place-names recorded by Ptolemy (A.D. 160) [see Hunter's *Orissa*, I. 310]. Of this migration Hiuen Tsang's name, Yavana (Yen-mo-na), for Cambodia, may be a trace [Beal's *Life of Hiuen Tsang*, xxxii]. A Saka invasion further explains Pausanias' (A.D. 170) name Sakaea for Cochin-China, and his description of the people as Skythians mixed with Indians. [Quoted in Bunbury's *Ancient Geography*, ii. 659. Bunbury suggests that Pausanias may have gained his information from Marcus Aurelius' (A.D. 166) ambassador to China.] There were fresh migrations during the fifth and sixth centuries, while among the deciphered Cambodian inscriptions there is evidence pointing to a Brahman dynasty, whose local initial date is in the early years of the seventh century, and one of whose kings, Somasarman (A.D. 610), is recorded to have held daily Mahabharata readings in the temples [Barth in *Jour. Asiatique*, ser. vi, tom. xix, p. 150, and *ibid.* x, 57, quoted in *Bombay Gazetteer*, vol. i, part i].

From Java the Hindus colonised Banjor Massin in Borneo, which was probably the most eastern of Hindu settlements [*J. R. A. S.* iv, 185]. Temples of superior workmanship with Hindu figures also occur at Waahoo, 400 miles from the coast [Dalton's *Diaks of Bourneo*, *Jour. Asiatique* (N.S.), vii, 153].

which in its Mahāyanist form and development was accepted by Tibet, Nepal and China with the neighbouring countries, as also parts of Farther India and Java, and in its Hīnayāna form gained, besides the countries of Farther India and Ceylon, Burma, Siam and Cambodia. This propagation of Indian thought and institutions was undoubtedly the work of countless colonists and missionaries, carried on through centuries, whose zeal must have been fed by a rich and stable national self-consciousness developed on a common soil and country. The colonising movement was (and always is) but the crest of a wave of popular enthusiasm for the country created and sustained by the realisation of its individuality and sacredness, a profound appreciation of all that it stands for, its ideals and institutions.

XXXII

We have now seen how in the past both religion and political experience contributed to the growth of a geographical sense in the people and to the perception of the fundamental unity of India behind her continental vastness and variety. The whole of the country was thus easily and naturally grasped by the national thought as a geographical unit whose strength and fervour triumphed over the physical difficulties of pre-mechanical ages in the way of having an intimate knowledge of the different parts which were welded into a whole. It was in a real sense the conquest of matter by mind; the subjection of the physical to the spiritual. India as a whole was realised as the mighty motherland by the popular mind in every part of India in spite of an unfavouring natural environment.

In modern times, the age of the improvement of transport, when the whole world has, so to say, been made smaller in size and is being centralised by railways, telegraphs and electrical machinery, when the ocean itself has been converted from a barrier into a broad highway of international intercourse, we can more easily and naturally realise the geographical unity of the whole of India. And besides, is not this unity apparent on the map? That country is geographically one of which the barriers separating its parts are less obstructive than those which isolate the area as a whole from surrounding regions. It is quite evident, and he who runs may read it, that India pre-eminently satisfies this test of unity. The great barrier of the north formed by the Himalayas, which may be easily rendered impregnable, effectually isolates the country from the rest of Asia, giving protection to it along a frontier of 2,000 miles, while towards the south the advantages of an insular position are secured by the sea. Thus sea-girt and mountain-guarded India is indisputably a geographical unit.

As regards any insurmountable internal barriers, we hardly come across one. The Himalayas overlook the great plain, the Indo-Gangetic depression which covers an area larger than France, Germany and Austria put together, and supports more than one-half of the total population of India. This is the region of which Sir Richard Strachey has said: "It is no exaggeration to say that it is possible to go from the Bay of Bengal up the Ganges through the Panjab and down the Indus again to the sea over a distance of 2,000 miles and more without finding a pebble, however small." The whole region is of one uniform level, one continuous stretch of land uninterrupted by any barrier, covered with a network of rivers, railways and canals, where one sees only "unbroken continents of wheat, millet and

Indian corn, endless seas of rice and limitless prairies of sugar-cane and indigo," an evidence of agricultural wealth oppressive almost in its monotony. Nor is the Vindhya or Satpura range any serious barrier obstructing communication between northern and southern India. Scarcely rising more than 4,000 feet above sea-level, both the ranges are now pierced by road and railway, and did not even in the earlier ages seriously interfere with the spread of Indo-Aryan civilisation, the diffusion of Hindu culture and learning to the parts of India lying to their south which are, equally with the north, the great stronghold of Hinduism.

Lastly, among other natural features which distinguish India from other countries may be mentioned the seasonal winds or monsoons which have stamped on the whole country a unique aspect. They have created those hydrographical conditions which have made of India pre-eminently the land of agriculture and one of the best-watered regions of the world. The census reports show that about 73 per cent. of the total population of India is dependent on agriculture for livelihood. While it may also be ascertained from statistics that, out of a total of 226 million acres annually sown in British India, only 44 million acres lack the natural water-supply and have to be artificially irrigated by the contrivances of man. So that fully 80 per cent. of the total area sown is naturally irrigated by the rivers of India pouring down in their bounty the streams of plenty. There also stands out, as the result of the operation of physical causes, the broad fundamental and distinguishing fact that Indian civilisation has developed and rests mainly on a rice-basis and the national diet is practically vegetarian.

XXXIII

Thus has India been helped both by nature and nurture, by her geographical conditions and historic experience, by her religious ideas and political ideals, to realise herself as a unit, to perceive, preserve and promote her individuality in fulfilment of her heaven-appointed mission in the culture-history of the world. Indian thought occupies a distinct place in the evolution of human thought; Indian life has its distinctive part to play in the history of humanity. Human culture would be incomplete and poor without its Indian contribution. The world is in need of India, a living, rejuvenated India—of the strength of her message, her cult, her faith. For what does India represent? "Not Universal Empire of the type attempted by the Eternal City, not Universal Spiritual Dominion like the Mother of all the

Churches." India's gift to the world has been the fair fabric of an Empire,[1] a Nationality, founded on the basis of Universal Peace (*Ahińsā*, अहिंसा), peace between man and man, and between man and every sentient creature; a fabric that was alas! ruthlessly shattered by the shock and collision of historic forces. For the Prime Maker of all history has perhaps ordained that the world should pass through the process of a painful historic development from the brute to the man.

Standing alone now in the background of historic nationalities and teeming millions, India calls us to the Cult of the Spirit, calls the mighty nations of the earth to lay down their pride and hate, their sceptres and swords, and, with redemptive humility, love and sacrifice, to fight in union the forces of rebarbarisation

[1] *E.g.*, the famous edicts of Asoka fully set forth the principles of *Ahińsā* and wide catholicity on which his great Empire was governed.

that are fast turning whole continents into armed hostile camps. It is in that Indian Cult of the Spirit that Nations, like Individuals, will find their rest and peace and realise the democratic dreams of a World Federation or a Parliament of Man.[1]

[1] This section is adapted from Dr. Brajendranath Seal's address to the First Universal Races Congress, London.

FINIS